This is the Hour

The Urgency of Living for Christ Now

Dr. Marcus Peter

En Route Books and Media, LLC
Saint Louis, MO

ENROUTE
Make the time

En Route Books and Media, LLC
5705 Rhodes Avenue
St. Louis, MO 63109

Contact us at
contactus@enroutebooksandmedia.com

Cover Credit: Marcus Peter

Copyright 2026 Marcus Peter

ISBN-13: 979-8-88870-534-6
Library of Congress Control Number: 2026940248

All rights reserved. No part of this book may be reproduced, stored in a retrieval system, or transmitted in any form, or by any means, electronic, mechanical, photocopying, or otherwise, without the prior written permission of the author.

Table of Contents

Introduction

What is the "hour?" When Jesus speaks of "the hour" in the Gospel of John, in His mouth that phrase gathers the whole purpose of His coming into the world and presses it into one blazing reality that stretches from the mystery of the Incarnation to the hill of Calvary and onward into the empty tomb and then into the cloud of Ascension glory, so that what sounds at first like a simple expression soon opens into the deepest center of salvation history. Early in John's Gospel, Our Lord says to His Mother at Cana, "My hour has not yet come" (John 2:4), and with those words He gives us a key that unlocks His mission; every sign He performs, every confrontation He endures, every act of mercy He extends, and every word He speaks is moving toward an appointed fulfillment known fully by Him and held securely within the will of His Father.

Therefore, the hour is the divinely appointed fulfillment of the Son's earthly mission through His suffering, crucifixion, Resurrection, and Ascension, and yet even that statement only begins to touch the depth of the matter, because this hour is also the hour of covenant fulfillment, the hour of sacrifice, the hour of priesthood, the hour of judgment upon sin, the hour of victory over death, the hour of the birth of the Church, and the hour in which heaven's saving purpose enters human history with irreversible force. St. John shows us repeatedly that Christ lives with full awareness of this coming fulfillment, since we read that hostile men could not seize Him "because his hour had not yet come" (John 7:30), and again that no one arrested Him in the temple "because his hour had not yet come" (John 8:20), which means that Jesus is never driven by events and never overtaken by enemies and never cornered by circumstances, as He is steadily advancing toward the sacred culmination for which He took flesh.

Then, as Jerusalem tightens around Him and the shadow of the Cross lengthens, Jesus declares, "The hour has come for the Son of man to be glorified" (John 12:23), and suddenly we begin to understand that glory in the Gospel is bound up with suffering and enthronement is bound up with sacrifice and divine triumph is bound up with the lifting up of the Son upon the wood of execution, so that what human eyes would call humiliation becomes in truth the revelation of the deepest splendor of divine love. Shortly after this, during the Last Supper, St. John writes with solemn simplicity, "Jesus knew that his hour had come to depart out of this world to the Father" (John 13:1), and, thus, the hour becomes the great passage of the true Passover Lamb who offers Himself in love and goes through death into life and opens the way for His people to follow.

The entire history of Israel had already prepared hearts and minds for an appointed hour of divine action through the long pedagogy of covenant, sacrifice, kingship, priesthood, and hope. The Exodus itself had an hour when the Lord passed through Egypt in judgment and mercy and when the blood of the lamb marked out a people for deliverance, as Exodus 12 recounts in vivid and terrible holiness, and that night shaped Jewish memory forever because redemption came through sacrifice and liberation came through blood and the people of God were brought forth through the mighty intervention of the Lord. Later at Sinai the covenant was ratified through sacrificial blood, for Moses took the blood and cast it upon the people and said, "Behold the blood of the covenant which the

Lord has made with you" (Exodus 24:8), so from the beginning Israel knew that covenant and blood belonged together and that fellowship with God was no casual arrangement and no sentimental bond and no merely interior aspiration; covenant was always solemn, objective, sacrificial, and binding.

Furthermore, the whole temple order trained Israel to live in expectation of a decisive act of divine redemption that would gather together sacrifice, priesthood, forgiveness, and holy presence. Day after day lambs were offered. Year after year the Day of Atonement returned. Generation after generation the people waited, prayed, sinned, repented, wandered, and hoped. The prophets deepened that expectation with words that grew more piercing over time, especially when Isaiah spoke of the Servant who would be "wounded for our transgressions" and upon whom "the Lord has laid… the iniquity of us all" (Isaiah 53:5–6), because here Israel was given a portrait of redemptive suffering that exceeded ordinary political hopes and reached into the mystery of a righteous one bearing the sins of many. Likewise, Daniel spoke of an appointed time and of a kingdom given by God, while Zechariah spoke of the one whom "they have pierced" and of a fountain opened "to cleanse them from sin and uncleanness" (Zechariah 12:10; 13:1), and, thus, the scriptural imagination of Israel was gradually formed for a redeeming act of God that would bring cleansing, judgment, sorrow, healing, and restored communion.

Jewish anticipation in the centuries surrounding the coming of Christ was, therefore, full of longing for deliverance, restoration, purification, kingship, and divine visitation, even if many did not yet perceive how all these hopes would converge in one suffering and triumphant Messiah. Some expected a royal son of David who would cast down oppressors. Some longed for a purified temple and a renewed priesthood. Some waited for the day of the Lord with trembling and hope. Some ached for the end of exile in its deepest spiritual sense. Into that longing Jesus came, and He did so as priest and victim and king and bridegroom and temple and Passover Lamb and Son of Man and obedient Son, which means that the hour He announces is the hour when all these rivers meet.

This matters profoundly because without the hour of Christ the Bible is nothing but a magnificent story whose center has yet to be unveiled, and human suffering is a riddle without its healing key, and sin is an accusation without its atoning answer, and death is a king whose dominion seems final, and religious striving is a weary reaching toward a communion we cannot secure by our own strength. Yet in the hour of Jesus all these things are drawn together and fulfilled. The Cross is the altar of the New Covenant. The Resurrection is the vindication of the Son and the breaking open of the grave. The Ascension is the enthronement of the victorious Christ who brings our humanity into the heavenly sanctuary. Therefore, the hour is one great mystery with several inseparable dimensions, and this book will keep those dimensions together because the Gospel itself keeps them together.

Moreover this theme matters personally because many Christians live as though the decisive act of God belongs mainly to the past while their daily lives belong mainly to habit, anxiety, distraction, private wounds, familiar temptations, and small ambitions, and, thus, the Christian life can slowly shrink into moral maintenance or religious background noise or occasional devotion when in truth the risen and ascended Lord has already acted decisively and now summons every baptized soul into urgent covenant fidelity. This is why the subject of the hour is no narrow topic for specialists and no merely literary theme and no decorative theological phrase. It reaches into every aspect of Christian life and, arguably, human existence.

Indeed, the language of the hour should unsettle us in a holy way, because Jesus entered His appointed fulfillment with full intention and complete love while many of us drift through days as if grace will always wait upon our indecision and as if repentance can be deferred without consequence and as if lukewarm discipleship is sufficient for a crucified and risen King. Scripture gives no support for such spiritual delay. St. Paul says, "Behold, now is the acceptable time; behold, now is the day of salvation" (2 Corinthians 6:2), and in that apostolic cry one hears the echo of Christ's own urgency. The hour of Jesus has inaugurated the hour of decision for us. Since He has died, risen, and ascended, the Christian life can never be casual.

Accordingly, this book seeks to walk through the great saving mystery of Christ's hour in a way that is biblically rooted, covenantally rich, spiritually searching, and personally compelling. We will begin at the Cross because the hour of redemptive suffering discloses the love of God with stunning force and reveals the true horror of sin and the true cost of our redemption. We will then move into the Resurrection because the hour of Christ does not end in burial and grief and silence precisely because the Father raises the Son in power and opens a new creation within history. From there we will look toward the Ascension because the Lord who rose also reigns, and His bodily entrance into heavenly glory means that our humanity has been carried into the presence of the Father and that the Church now lives beneath the lordship of the enthroned Christ. Finally, we will ask what all this means for us now, because doctrine is given for discipleship and revelation is given for conversion and truth is given for communion.

In that sense this book is about urgency, though by urgency I do not mean panic or frenzy or strained religious activism, because the Gospel produces something far deeper and steadier and more searching. I mean the urgency that comes when a soul finally understands that Christ has acted decisively and that every human life now unfolds under the light of His finished work and living reign. I mean the urgency that awakens when one sees that time is holy and that one's body belongs to the Lord and that one's vocation is a real participation in the covenant life of grace. I mean the urgency of repentance and adoration and obedience and sacramental life and mission. I mean the sober joy of knowing that Christ has opened heaven and that He deserves our whole selves.

For that reason, the "hour" matters to all of us personally. It matters because many souls are tired and distracted and spiritually divided. It matters because many believers know pieces of the Gospel while living far from its burning center. It matters because modern life forms us toward speed and vanity and fragmentation while the hour of Christ gathers us into worship and fidelity and hope. It matters because the Church in every age must return again to the pierced side of Christ and to the empty tomb and to the hill of Ascension if she is to live with fire and conviction and endurance. It matters because Jesus entered the hour for us.

So then, what is the hour? It is the appointed fulfillment of the Son's mission. It is the covenant hour. It is the sacrificial hour. It is the redeeming hour. It is the victorious hour. It is the hour in which the Lamb is slain, death begins to die, and heaven opens over humanity. It is the hour that reveals divine love in its fiercest beauty. It is the hour that compels a response. And since that hour has come and its power abides forever through the living Christ, this book is an invitation to step out of delay and into the blazing heart of the Gospel.

Chapter 1

The Hour of the Cross

When Our Lord said, "My soul is very sorrowful, even to death" (Mt 26:38, RSVCE), He drew His disciples toward the dreadful holiness of the hour for which He had come. Earlier in the Gospel of John, Jesus repeatedly spoke of His "hour" as something appointed by the Father and moving steadily toward fulfillment. At Cana He said, "My hour has not yet come" (Jn 2:4, RSVCE). In Jerusalem, amid mounting hostility, St. John tells us that no one laid hands on Him "because his hour had not yet come" (Jn 7:30, RSVCE; cf. Jn 8:20, RSVCE). Then, as Holy Week opens and the shadow of Calvary lengthens across the city, Jesus finally declares, "The hour has come for the Son of man to be glorified" (Jn 12:23, RSVCE). Therefore, the Cross is never an accident of history. It is the appointed hour of covenant fulfillment, sacrificial love, priestly self-offering, and victorious obedience.

Christ went to Golgotha knowingly, deliberately, and lovingly. He says, "For this purpose I have come to this hour" (Jn 12:27, RSVCE). That sentence alone should shake every casual soul awake. The Son of God took flesh for this hour. He preached for this hour. He healed for this hour. He gathered disciples for this hour. He entered Jerusalem for this hour. Accordingly, when we gaze upon the Cross, we behold the center of history and the furnace of divine love. We behold the place where everything promised in shadow begins to blaze in fulfillment.

Sacred Scripture presents the death of Christ as atonement, sacrifice and the triumph of obedient love. St. Paul writes with terrible beauty, "Christ, our paschal lamb, has been sacrificed" (1 Cor 5:7, RSVCE). Likewise, St. Peter declares, "You were ransomed from the futile ways inherited from your fathers, not with perishable things such as silver or gold, but with the precious blood of Christ, like that of a lamb without blemish or spot" (1 Pet 1:18–19, RSVCE). Here one begins to see the inner grammar of redemption. Israel was delivered by the blood of the lamb at Passover (Ex 12:1–14, RSVCE). Sinai was sealed through sacrificial blood when Moses took the blood and said, "Behold the blood of the covenant which the Lord has made with you" (Ex 24:8, RSVCE). Therefore, when Christ takes the chalice and says, "This is my blood of the covenant, which is poured out for many for the forgiveness of sins" (Mt 26:28, RSVCE), He gathers Exodus, sacrifice, priesthood, and covenant into Himself.

The Cross is the Hour

The Cross, therefore, is the hour when the New Covenant is ratified in the Blood of the Son. The Catechism teaches that "Jesus' redemptive death fulfills Isaiah's prophecy of the suffering Servant" and that He "atoned for our faults and made satisfaction for our sins to the Father" (CCC 615). It also teaches that Jesus "gave the supreme expression of his free offering of himself at the meal shared with the twelve Apostles" and that "the sacrifice of Christ and the sacrifice of the Eucharist are one single sacrifice" (CCC 610, 1367). Consequently, Calvary is no bare display of pain. It is the priestly self-offering of the incarnate Son who gives Himself to the Father for us and for our salvation. As Hebrews proclaims, "Christ entered, once for all, into the Holy Place, taking not the blood of goats and calves but his own blood, thus securing an eternal redemption" (Heb 9:12, RSVCE).

This means that the hour of the Cross reveals the very heart of God. Jesus Himself says, "Greater love has no man than this, that a man lay down his life for his friends" (Jn 15:13, RSVCE). Yet the wonder grows deeper still, for St. Paul writes, "God shows his love for us in that while we were yet sinners Christ died for us" (Rom 5:8, RSVCE). He loved us amid rebellion. He sought us amid estrangement. He embraced the wood of death so that sons and daughters might enter the household of divine life. In this light the Cross becomes intensely personal. One cannot hide behind crowds, epochs, or abstract categories. He died for us. He loved us. He offered Himself for us. St. Paul says it with astonishing intimacy: "The Son of God… loved me and gave himself for me" (Gal 2:20, RSVCE). Those words ought to remove every excuse for our spiritual distance.

Moreover, the Cross unveils the horror of sin. Modern man often treats evil as malfunction, social friction, therapeutic imbalance, or the residue of flawed systems. Yet Calvary reveals sin as revolt against God, rupture within the covenant, and a wound so grave that only the Blood of the incarnate Son could heal it. The Catechism states, "Sinners were the authors and the ministers of all the sufferings that the divine Redeemer endured" (CCC 598). Therefore, one cannot approach the Passion with detached curiosity. One approaches with repentance. One approaches with grief. One approaches with gratitude. One approaches with awe. St. Augustine says, "God loved us even when we practiced enmity toward Him and committed wickedness" (*Confessions*, X.43). That insight reaches deeply into the human heart. The Cross shows both what sin costs and what mercy gives.

Christ is the New Adam

Furthermore, the hour of the Cross reveals Christ as the new Adam whose obedience heals Adam's disobedience. St. Paul writes, "For as by one man's disobedience many were made sinners, so by one man's obedience many will be made righteous" (Rom 5:19, RSVCE). The first Adam reached for false exaltation through disobedience. The new Adam humbled Himself through obedient love "unto death, even death on a cross" (Phil 2:8, RSVCE). Therefore, the tree of death becomes the tree of life. St. Irenaeus saw this mystery with luminous depth: "The knot of Eve's disobedience was loosed by the obedience of Mary" and Christ "recapitulated in Himself the long history of mankind" (*Against Heresies*, III.22.4; III.18.1). The Cross, then, gathers humanity's shattered story into the obedient Body of the Son and opens a renewed human future within grace.

Here one must also speak of priesthood, because the Cross is the supreme priestly act of Christ. Hebrews says, "Although he was a Son, he learned obedience through what he suffered; and being made perfect he became the source of eternal salvation to all who obey him" (Heb 5:8–9, RSVCE). Again, "We have a great high priest who has passed through the heavens, Jesus, the Son of God" (Heb 4:14, RSVCE). His priesthood reaches fulfillment precisely in self-offering. He is a priest, altar, and victim. The Catechism teaches,

"The whole of Christ's life was a continual teaching: his silences, his miracles, his gestures, his prayer, his love for people, his special affection for the little and the poor, the acceptance of the total sacrifice on the cross for the redemption of the world" (CCC 561). Therefore, the Cross is the fullest sermon Christ ever preached. The Cross is the Gospel revealing His covenant love unto the end.

Satan is Defeated

In addition, the hour of the Cross is the hour in which Satan's apparent triumph collapses into defeat. Jesus announces before His Passion, "Now is the judgment of this world, now shall the ruler of this world be cast out" (Jn 12:31, RSVCE). What looked like victory for darkness became the crushing of the serpent through the pierced heel of the promised Seed (Gen 3:15, RSVCE). St. John Chrysostom exulted over this mystery when he preached that the devil "took a body, and discovered God; he took earth, and encountered heaven" (*Paschal Homily*). Indeed, the enemy sought to consume Christ through death, and instead death itself began to die from within. The Cross, therefore, is warfare, though of a holy and astonishing kind. Christ conquers by surrender. He reigns by offering. He overthrows the ancient tyrant by perfect fidelity to the Father.

Yet the Cross also judges every cheap view of discipleship. Jesus said plainly, "If any man would come after me, let him deny himself and take up his cross daily and follow me" (Lk 9:23, RSVCE). This means that Christian life can never be reduced to sentiment, cultural association, inherited memory, or occasional inspiration. Covenant life always includes sacrifice, fidelity, endurance, and loving obedience. The Catechism teaches, "The way of perfection passes by way of the Cross. There is no holiness without renunciation and spiritual battle" (CCC 2015). Therefore, the hour of Christ's Cross presses upon our own lives with grave urgency. If the Master entered glory through obedience and suffering, then the servant must learn to walk the same road with trust, humility, and perseverance.

The Cross Illuminates Our Reason

The Cross reveals what the greatest minds sought dimly through natural reason. Aristotle recognized that the highest friendship involves willing the good of another and living virtuously for the sake of the good (*Nicomachean Ethics*, VIII.2, 1155b31–1156a5). Yet at Calvary one sees divine charity enter history and give itself for the undeserving. Likewise, Plato longed for the just man who would remain righteous even under terrible suffering and public humiliation (*Republic*, II.361e–362a). In Christ one beholds the perfectly just One condemned, scourged, mocked, pierced, and offered up in love. Philosophy asks its highest questions about justice, goodness, friendship, sacrifice, and the highest human end. The Cross of Christ is its highest answer.

St. Thomas Aquinas, drawing these streams into Christian wisdom, teaches that Christ's Passion was fitting because through it man comes to know both the gravity of sin and the greatness of divine love, and through it he is stirred toward holiness (*Summa Theologiae*, III, q. 46, a. 3). That is profoundly important. The Passion does not merely achieve something objectively outside us, though it surely does. It also transforms the human person inwardly. It awakens repentance. It inflames love. It strengthens hope. It trains the heart toward virtue. In this way the Cross becomes a school, sanctuary, battlefield, and a home for the soul.

Then one must ask what happened in the heart of the Blessed Virgin during this hour. Simeon had foretold, "A sword will pierce through your own soul also" (Lk 2:35, RSVCE). At Calvary, that prophecy ripens in sorrow and fidelity. Vatican II speaks of Mary who "faithfully persevered in her union with her Son unto the cross" (*Lumen Gentium* 58). She remained, entrusting herself wholly to the Father's mysterious work in the very midst of agony. Thus, Mary becomes, in a profoundly maternal way, an icon of covenant fidelity beneath the shadow of sacrifice. And from the Cross Jesus gives her as mother to the beloved disciple, saying, "Behold, your mother!" (Jn 19:27, RSVCE). Even in the hour of death He forms a household, gathering His covenant family to Himself.

The Birth of the Church

The Church herself comes forth from this hour. The Catechism teaches, "The Church was born primarily of Christ's total self-giving for our salvation, anticipated in the institution of the Eucharist and fulfilled on the cross" (CCC 766). St. John's Gospel records that blood and water flowed from the pierced side of Christ (Jn 19:34, RSVCE), and the Fathers saw here a sign of sacramental life pouring forth for the Church. St. Augustine wrote, "The Evangelist has used a well-chosen word. He did say pierced, or wounded, or anything else, but 'opened,' so that thereby there was opened the gate of life"

(*Tractates on the Gospel of John*, 120.2). Therefore, the hour of the Cross is also the hour of ecclesial birth. From the wounded Bridegroom comes forth the Bride. From the opened side comes living water, cleansing blood, sacramental grace, and covenant communion.

This also means that every Eucharist returns us to this holy hour. The Church does not repeat Calvary as though Christ suffered again and again. Rather, the one sacrifice is made sacramentally present in the liturgy. The Catechism states, "In the liturgy of the Church, it is principally his own Paschal mystery that Christ signifies and makes present" (CCC 1085). Again, "As often as the sacrifice of the Cross by which 'Christ our Pasch has been sacrificed' is celebrated on the altar, the work of our redemption is carried out" (CCC 1364, quoting *Lumen Gentium* 3). Therefore, Christian urgency grows from the altar. We do not manufacture zeal through emotional intensity. We receive divine life from the Lamb once slain, now risen and glorified, who gives us His Body and Blood.

The Demand of the Cross

So then, what does this hour demand from us? First, repentance. When St. Peter preached Christ crucified, his hearers "were cut to the heart" (Acts 2:37, RSVCE). Such cutting is mercy. It tears through self-deception and brings the sinner toward life. Second, faith. One must trust the crucified Christ wholly, personally, and perseveringly. Third, surrender. St. Paul says, "You are not your own; you were bought with a price" (1 Cor 6:19–20, RSVCE). Covenant life, therefore, means belonging. Fourth, love. "We love, because he first loved us" (1 Jn 4:19, RSVCE). The Cross summons forth a life poured out in return. Fifth, endurance. "Let us run with perseverance the race that is set before us, looking to Jesus the pioneer and perfecter of our faith" (Heb 12:1–2, RSVCE). In other words, the hour of the Cross reaches into the present and lays claim upon every faculty of our being.

Dear friend, the Cross is far too holy for decorative admiration and far too glorious for occasional religious sentiment. Christ's hour has entered history forever. Therefore, every human life now unfolds under the sign of Calvary. Every ambition, wound, grief, temptation, attachment, and desire must come under the lordship of the crucified King. The world urges haste toward vanity. The flesh urges retreat into comfort. The devil urges forgetfulness. Yet the Son of God, lifted up for us, draws all things toward Himself (Jn 12:32, RSVCE). He summons us to a covenant fidelity, demanding our whole life.

For this reason, the hour of the Cross is also your hour of decision. Moses once said to Israel, "I have set before you life and death, blessing and curse; therefore choose life" (Deut 30:19, RSVCE). That ancient covenant summons reaches its blazing fullness at Golgotha.

Choose life in the Crucified One.
Choose forgiveness through His Blood.
Choose sonship through His obedience.
Choose sanctity through His grace.
Choose the Church born from His side.

Choose the Eucharist that makes present His sacrifice.
Choose the road that leads through surrender into glory.

Christ has already entered the hour. He has already loved unto the end. He has already shed the Blood of the Covenant. Therefore, delay becomes spiritually dangerous. Lukewarmness becomes intolerable. Evasion becomes tragic. The Cross says that God has acted decisively. The Cross says that salvation has been opened. The Cross says that time itself has been marked by redeeming love. Therefore, this is the hour to kneel, the hour to repent, the hour to believe, the hour to return, the hour to forgive, the hour to renounce sin, the hour to adore, and the hour to live wholly for Jesus Christ.

And so we begin here, at the foot of the Cross, where heaven stoops toward earth and mercy pours through wounded flesh. Here the covenant is sealed. Here the Lamb is offered. Here the Church is born. This is where the soul learns love. This is the hour of the Cross, and through this hour every other hour of Christian life receives its meaning.

Meditation Questions

1. When I look upon the Cross, do I truly believe that Christ "loved me and gave himself for me" (Gal. 2:20), or have I allowed the Passion to become familiar and distant?
2. In what areas of my life have I grown spiritually casual, slow to repent, or resistant to full surrender to the Lordship of Jesus?

3. What sins, attachments, habits, resentments, or private compromises does the hour of the Cross now expose in my conscience?
4. Do I approach Calvary merely as an event to admire, or as the covenant sacrifice through which I have been bought "with a price" (1 Cor. 6:20)?
5. How does the wounded love of Christ reshape the way I understand suffering, sacrifice, obedience, and holiness in my own vocation?
6. Have I received the mercy of God deeply enough to become more merciful toward others, especially those who have wounded me?
7. What does it mean, concretely and immediately, for me to take up my cross daily and follow Christ in this season of life?
8. Do I live as though time is sacred and charged with eternal significance, or do I still treat my days as though I have endless chances to delay conversion?
9. How often do I unite my own sorrows, labors, disappointments, and hidden sacrifices to the Cross of Christ?
10. Am I living as a member of the Church born from the pierced side of Christ, with love for her sacraments, her worship, and her covenant life?
11. Has the Eucharist become for me the living center of my week, my prayer, my repentance, and my identity?
12. If Christ entered His hour with love and obedience, what is the hour of obedience He is asking of me right now?

Spiritual Call to Action

This truth should lead toward response. The Cross of Christ demands an answer. Therefore, over the next seven days, make this reality concrete in prayer and action.

First, spend at least fifteen minutes each day in silence before a crucifix. Read slowly one Passion text from the Gospels, especially Matthew 26 to 27, Mark 14 to 15, Luke 22 to 23, or John 18 to 19. Then say plainly to the Lord: Jesus, show me what in my life still resists Your Cross.

Second, make a serious examination of conscience. Name your sins honestly. Name your evasions honestly. Name your spiritual laziness honestly. Then go to sacramental confession as soon as reasonably possible. Do not delay. The hour of the Cross is an hour of mercy.

Third, attend Mass with renewed intention, especially if you can do so on a weekday. When the Holy Eucharist is elevated, consciously unite your whole life to Christ's sacrifice, including your fears, griefs, desires, responsibilities, and hidden sufferings.

Fourth, choose one concrete act of self-denial this week. It may be fasting, restraint in speech, giving up unnecessary comfort, rising earlier for prayer, or turning away from a recurring indulgence. Offer it in union with the Cross for a specific intention.

Fifth, reconcile where reconciliation is possible. If there is someone you need to forgive, contact, or pray for seriously, begin there. The Blood of the Covenant should reshape the heart.

Finally, pray this each day:

Lord Jesus Christ, You entered Your hour for me.
You loved me unto the end.
You shed the Blood of the Covenant for my salvation.
Draw me out of delay, compromise, and half-heartedness.
Teach me to repent sincerely, to love deeply, and to follow You faithfully.
Let the hour of Your Cross become the measure of my life.
Amen.

Chapter 2

The Dawn of the Resurrection

The hour of the Cross leads straight into the dawn of the Resurrection, and unless we enter that dawn with reverence and trembling gratitude, we will hear the Gospel only in fragments and receive the Christian life only in reduced form, because the crucified Christ rose bodily from the grave and in rising He transformed history, sanctified hope, vindicated every word He spoke, and opened for His people a living future that death itself can never seal again. Therefore, I begin here where the women began, with grief still near, with spices prepared, with love still searching, and with the earth already changed forever through an act of divine power whose glory exceeds every created image.

St. John writes beautifully, "On the first day of the week Mary Magdalene came to the tomb early, while it was still dark" (Jn 20:1, RSVCE), and that phrase, "while it was still dark," communicates that darkness had settled upon the disciples through loss and fear and bewilderment and shattered expectation, while the powers of this world had already done their fiercest work against the Son of God, and yet precisely there, before dawn fully spread across the land, Christ had already risen. Thus, Christian hope begins here, with God acting in salvation history long before human hearts have gathered themselves to Him.

The Resurrection, therefore, is no appendix to the Passion. It is the Father's glorious answer to the obedient self-offering of the Son. St. Paul says, "He was put to death for our trespasses and raised for our justification" (Rom 4:25, RSVCE). Again, he declares, "If Christ has not been raised, your faith is futile and you are still in your sins" (1 Cor 15:17, RSVCE). The entire Christian proclamation turns upon this. If Jesus remained in the grave, then His claims collapse into memory and His Cross becomes a tragedy without triumph and His promises lose their force. Yet because He rose, everything changes. The Catechism says, "The Resurrection of Jesus is the crowning truth of our faith in Christ, a faith believed and lived as the central truth by the first Christian community" (CCC 638). Thus, the dawn of Easter is the crowning truth through which the Church lives her entire existence.

The Covenant Anticipates the Resurrection

Moreover, the Resurrection is deeply covenantal, because God had bound Himself to His people through promise after promise, oath after oath, sign after sign, and those promises were moving toward a victorious heir of David, a true Shepherd, a righteous Servant, a holy Son, and a redeeming Lord whose reign would endure forever. Psalm 16 had already cried out, "For thou dost not give me up to Sheol, or let thy godly one see the Pit" (Ps 16:10, RSVCE). Isaiah had proclaimed concerning the suffering Servant that "he shall see his offspring, he shall prolong his days" (Is 53:10, RSVCE), which means that the servant who pours out his soul unto death also lives beyond death through the Lord's saving purpose. Hosea spoke prophetically, "After two days he will revive us; on the third day he will raise us up" (Hos 6:2, RSVCE). Jonah emerged alive on the third day from the deep, and Jesus Himself gave that sign interpretively to

His generation, saying, "As Jonah was three days and three nights in the belly of the whale, so will the Son of man be three days and three nights in the heart of the earth" (Mt 12:40, RSVCE). Therefore, the Resurrection is the flowering of ancient covenant hope.

Jewish anticipation also gives this dawn a richer horizon, because first century Jews had long lived with a robust expectation that God would finally act to vindicate the righteous, judge the wicked, renew Israel, raise the dead, and establish His kingdom with finality and glory. The Sadducees denied resurrection, as the Gospels make plain, yet many Jews, including the Pharisees, embraced a future resurrection of the dead grounded in texts such as Daniel 12:2, where we read, "And many of those who sleep in the dust of the earth shall awake" (RSVCE). Martha herself voices this expectation when she says of Lazarus, "I know that he will rise again in the resurrection at the last day" (Jn 11:24, RSVCE). Jesus answers her with a claim that gathers all Jewish hope into His own person, "I am the resurrection and the life" (Jn 11:25, RSVCE). Consequently, Easter morning is the eruption within history of the age to come. The general resurrection awaited at the end has begun in the body of Jesus Christ.

This truth matters profoundly because Christ rose bodily. The empty tomb is, therefore, essential. Christianity does not rest upon a merely interior consolation or a spiritualized survival or a noble remembrance cherished by disciples who wished to preserve His influence. The tomb was empty. He showed His wounds. He ate with them. He spoke with them. He invited Thomas, "Put your finger here, and see my hands; and put out your hand, and place it in my side" (Jn 20:27, RSVCE). St. Luke reports that the risen Jesus said, "See my hands and my feet, that it is I myself; handle me, and see;

for a spirit has not flesh and bones as you see that I have" (Lk 24:39, RSVCE). Therefore, the Resurrection confirms the goodness of creation, the dignity of the body, and the permanence of Christ's incarnate humanity. The Word who became flesh resurrected and glorified that same human nature.

The Catechism teaches this specifically, "The risen Jesus establishes direct contact with his disciples by letting them touch him and by sharing a meal with them" and "Jesus is no ghost" (CCC 645). It further teaches that Christ's risen body is "filled with the power of the Holy Spirit" and shares in divine glory while remaining truly physical and truly His own (CCC 646). This is essential for every Christian because salvation in Christ does not bypass our humanity. Grace heals and elevates human nature. Redemption reaches the body and the soul. The grave, therefore, loses its tyranny, because what has happened in the body of the Lord is the firstfruits of what shall happen in His people. St. Paul says, "Christ has been raised from the dead, the first fruits of those who have fallen asleep" (1 Cor 15:20, RSVCE). Again, "For as in Adam all die, so also in Christ shall all be made alive" (1 Cor 15:22, RSVCE).

The Resurrection is Personal

At this point the heart must slow down and receive the personal force of Easter. The Resurrection means that the love revealed on the Cross has truly triumphed. It means that every promise of Jesus is firm. It means that the Father received the Son's sacrifice with total delight. It means that sin has lost dominion over those united to Christ. It means that despair speaks falsely. It means that grief, though piercing and deep, never has the final word for those who belong to the risen Lord. When Mary Magdalene met Him in the garden, she first mistook Him for the gardener, until He said her name, "Mary" (Jn 20:16, RSVCE). Then everything changed through one word from the living Christ. So too, the Resurrection reaches each soul personally. Christ rises for His Church and also calls each disciple by name into living communion.

This is why the Fathers preach Easter with such fire. St. John Chrysostom exults, "Christ is risen, and life is liberated" (*Paschal Homily*). St. Augustine proclaims, "The resurrection of the Lord is our hope" (*Sermon* 261.1). These ancient voices speak with enduring force because Easter is the ground of Christian hope, and hope in Christian theology is never vague optimism or emotional brightness or cheerful denial of pain. Rather, hope is the theological virtue by which we desire the kingdom of heaven and eternal life as our happiness, trusting in Christ's promises and relying upon the help of grace rather than upon our own strength alone (CCC 1817). Thus, the Resurrection nourishes hope through objective victory. Christ truly rose. Therefore, hope rests upon that historical fact of divine glory.

Furthermore, Easter is the dawn of the new creation. St. John takes care to place the Resurrection "on the first day of the week" (Jn 20:1, RSVCE), and this is no incidental detail. The first creation began with light bursting into darkness at the word of God (Gen 1:3, RSVCE). The new creation begins with the Light of the world leaving the tomb in triumph after the darkness of Good Friday and Holy Saturday. Consequently, the Resurrection is cosmic in scope even as it is personal in tenderness. The one through whom all things were made now renews all things through His victory over death. The Catechism says, "The Resurrection of Christ is the principle and source of our future resurrection" (CCC 655). In addition, "Christ's Resurrection and the risen Christ himself are the principle and source of our future resurrection" (CCC 658). Therefore, Easter reaches beyond the consolation of the apostles and toward the restoration of creation itself.

St. Paul develops this with immense beauty in Romans and First Corinthians. "If any one is in Christ, he is a new creation" (2 Cor 5:17, RSVCE). "We were buried therefore with him by baptism into death, so that as Christ was raised from the dead by the glory of the Father, we too might walk in newness of life" (Rom 6:4, RSVCE). This means that Easter is not merely something to admire. It is something into which we are sacramentally incorporated. Baptism unites us to Christ's death and Resurrection. The old man is crucified with Him. Grace gives a new principle of life. Therefore, Christian urgency grows stronger here. Since Christ is risen and since we have died and risen with Him sacramentally, every compromise with sin becomes a contradiction of our baptismal identity. St. Paul presses the point with force, "So you also must consider yourselves dead to sin and alive to God in Christ Jesus" (Rom 6:11, RSVCE).

The Resurrection is Divine Justice

The Resurrection also vindicates divine justice in a profound way. At the Cross the world judged Jesus falsely. Religious authorities condemned Him. Imperial power executed Him. Mockery surrounded Him. Violence stripped Him. Yet Easter reveals the Father's verdict over the Son. Jesus is righteous. Jesus is beloved. Jesus is truly King. Jesus is Lord. Peter proclaims on Pentecost, "This Jesus God raised up, and of that we all are witnesses" (Acts 2:32, RSVCE), and shortly after he declares, "God raised him up, having loosed the pangs of death, because it was not possible for him to be held by it" (Acts 2:24, RSVCE). That phrase, "it was not possible," deserves deep meditation. Death had no rightful claim upon the Holy One. Corruption had no dominion over the sinless Son. The grave could receive Him for a short span within the mystery of redemption, yet it could never retain Him.

This matters because every great search for permanence, meaning, goodness, and the highest human end reaches a kind of threshold beyond which reason longs for light greater than itself. Plato's *Phaedo* wrestles with the soul's immortality and with death as a passage toward judgment and lasting truth. Aristotle teaches that every human action tends toward some good, while the highest good is that for the sake of which all else is pursued (*Nicomachean Ethics*, I.1, 1094a1–3; I.7, 1097b20–1098a20). These philosophical insights reach toward the human longing for abiding blessedness and final meaning. Easter answers these yearnings historically and personally in Christ, because the highest good is communion with the living God through the risen Son, and eternal life is no abstraction suspended above history as it has entered history bodily in the Resurrection of Jesus. St. Thomas Aquinas, therefore, teaches that Christ's Resurrection was necessary for the manifestation of divine justice, for the strengthening of our faith, for the raising of our hope, and for the ordering of our lives toward resurrectional things (*Summa Theologiae*, III, q. 53, a. 1).

Yet the dawn of the Resurrection also passes through wounded hearts. The disciples entered Easter in confusion, shame, fear, and grief. Peter had denied his Master. Thomas would wrestle with doubt. The road to Emmaus was traveled by men whose faces were downcast (Lk 24:17, RSVCE). This is spiritually decisive, because the risen Christ comes to real people amid collapse and bewilderment. He reveals Himself to those whose hope has been battered and whose courage has thinned. Therefore, the Resurrection speaks powerfully to every Christian soul that has endured sorrow, humiliation, repeated sin, spiritual fatigue, or seasons of interior darkness. Easter says that Christ enters precisely there and says, "Peace be with you" (Jn 20:19, RSVCE).

The Resurrection is Our Mission

Moreover, the Resurrection gives form to the Church's mission. Jesus says to the apostles, "As the Father has sent me, even so I send you" (Jn 20:21, RSVCE). Then He breathes on them and says, "Receive the Holy Spirit" (Jn 20:22, RSVCE). Here Easter morning reaches toward Pentecost and toward the sacramental life of the Church. The risen Christ forms a people, sends them into the world, grants them peace, and entrusts to them the ministry of forgiveness. The Catechism teaches that Jesus associated the apostles with His own mission and from the beginning prepared and formed them to continue His saving work (CCC 858–860). Therefore, the Resurrection is missionary. The Church proclaims a living Lord. She announces an empty tomb and a living Christ who reigns and gives mercy.

This also explains why Sunday became the Lord's Day. The Resurrection took place on the first day of the week. The Church, therefore, gathers each Sunday around the Eucharist in remembrance and presence of the Paschal mystery. St. Ignatius of Antioch speaks of Christians as those who live "according to the Lord's Day" (*Letter to the Magnesians* 9). The Catechism echoes this apostolic tradition and teaches that Sunday is the day of the Resurrection and the foundation and kernel of the whole liturgical year (CCC 1166–1167). Thus, Easter orders Christian time. It reorients weekly life. It teaches the baptized to live from the victory of Christ regularly and concretely. Each Sunday says again that death has been conquered and that the risen Lord gathers His people.

Easter Reorders Time Itself

Yet Easter also bears a sobering urgency. Because Christ is risen, time can never again be treated as spiritually neutral; because the tomb is empty, every day takes place beneath the light of the living Christ; because He has triumphed over sin and death, lukewarm discipleship becomes intolerably thin; and because baptism unites us to His risen life, we are summoned toward holiness with renewed seriousness. St. Paul, therefore, says, "If then you have been raised with Christ, seek the things that are above, where Christ is" (Col 3:1, RSVCE). He continues, "Set your minds on things that are above, not on things that are on earth" (Col 3:2, RSVCE). Easter, therefore, compels the reordering of every aspect of our life, practical and spiritual.

Dear friend, the dawn of the Resurrection is meant to enter your own life. Christ rose bodily, truly, gloriously, and for you. His victory is not distant from your wounds. His life is not unrelated to your fears. His triumph is not reserved for saints already perfected in glory. He comes into the locked rooms of ordinary disciples. He comes into households marked by grief. He comes into consciences marked by shame. He comes into vocations burdened by exhaustion. He comes into hearts that still tremble and says, "Peace be with you" (Jn 20:21, RSVCE). Then He does more: He sends. He heals. He feeds. He restores. He reorients. He gives a future. Therefore, Easter is deeply personal while also being gloriously cosmic.

And so the dawn of the Resurrection reveals the Father's vindication of the Son, the triumph of divine love, the opening of the new creation, the firstfruits of our own bodily resurrection, the healing of apostolic fear, the birth of missionary courage, and the sacramental pulse of the Church's life. This dawn teaches us that death is a defeated tyrant, that sin has lost its throne over those united to Christ, that hope has entered history with flesh and wounds transfigured by glory, and that the Christian life must now be lived with Easter seriousness and Easter joy. In the next chapter we will rise higher still, because the One who rose also ascended, and the dawn of Easter opens toward the enthronement of the Son whose risen humanity now enters the heavenly sanctuary for us.

Meditation Questions

1. When I hear that Christ is risen, do I receive that truth as the blazing center of my life, or has it become a familiar language that no longer pierces my heart?
2. Do I truly believe that the Resurrection was bodily, historical, victorious, and personal, and that it changes the meaning of my suffering, my fears, and my future?
3. What areas of my life still live as though the tomb were sealed, as though hope were weak, as though grace were distant?
4. In what ways have grief, disappointment, shame, fatigue, or old wounds narrowed my expectation of what the risen Christ can do in me?
5. Do I live from my baptism as one who has died and risen with Christ, as St. Paul teaches in Romans 6:4 and Colossians 3:1?
6. Have I allowed Easter to shape my weekly life through Sunday worship, or have I treated the Lord's Day casually?
7. When Jesus says, "Peace be with you" (John 20:19), what unrest, fear, or inward turmoil in me most needs to receive that word?
8. Am I seeking "the things that are above, where Christ is" (Colossians 3:1), or am I still overly bound to passing ambitions, distractions, and earthly attachments?
9. How does the Resurrection strengthen my understanding of the dignity of the body, the hope of eternal life, and the future resurrection of the faithful?

10. Have I let the risen Christ restore me in the places where I have failed Him, as He restored Peter after denial?
11. In what concrete way is the Resurrection calling me toward greater courage, greater purity, deeper prayer, and more joyful fidelity?
12. If the tomb is empty and Christ is alive, what excuse for spiritual delay still remains in me?

Spiritual Call to Action

This truth should draw the soul into Easter response and Easter discipline. The Resurrection is not merely to be admired. It is to be lived.

Therefore, for the next seven days, begin each morning by making the sign of the cross and praying slowly: Lord Jesus Christ, risen from the dead, make me live today as one who belongs to Your victory.

Then read one Resurrection passage each day. Move prayerfully through Matthew 28, Mark 16, Luke 24, John 20, John 21, 1 Corinthians 15, and Colossians 3. Read slowly. Stay with the words. Let them enter your conscience and your imagination. Ask the Lord to show you where your life still behaves as though He were absent.

Next, make one concrete act each day that reflects resurrectional living. Reach out to someone you have neglected. Begin a delayed duty. Renounce one recurring sin firmly and deliberately. Return to disciplined prayer. Bring order to one area of your life that has drifted into spiritual laziness. Do something that says with your actions that Christ is alive and reigns.

Also, renew your baptismal identity consciously. If possible, place your hand in holy water at church and say: Jesus, You have joined me to Your death and Resurrection. Teach me to live as a new creation. If you are unable to go to church that day, still pray those words with intention.

Then, attend Mass this week with special attention to the risen Christ who gathers His people. If Sunday is approaching, prepare for it seriously. Guard it. Enter it reverently. Give the Lord's Day back its proper place. Let Sunday become the weekly shape of your hope.

Finally, identify one fear that has ruled you recently and place it explicitly before the risen Lord. Name it in prayer. Then say aloud: Christ is risen. Therefore, this fear is not my master.

You may close each day with this prayer:

Risen Lord Jesus,
You entered the grave and shattered its dominion.
You rose in glory and opened the future of life for Your people.
Enter the dark places in me with Your holy light.
Restore what has grown weak in me.
Strengthen what has grown fearful in me.
Raise what has grown tired in me.
Teach me to live as one baptized into Your victory.
Let Your Resurrection govern my thoughts, my desires, my choices, and my hope.
Amen.

Chapter 3

The Throne of the Ascended Christ

The dawn of the Resurrection opens upward into the glory of the Ascension, because the risen Jesus also returns to the Father in His glorified humanity and takes His seat in heavenly majesty, and through that royal exaltation He draws the whole Church into a new relation with God, with history, with worship, with mission, and with hope. Therefore, the Ascension is no brief farewell tucked away at the edge of the Gospel story. Rather, it is the enthronement of the crucified and risen Lord, the public vindication of His kingship, the heavenly presentation of His redeeming work, and the opening of a new and living access for His people into the presence of the Father.

St. Luke writes, "Then he led them out as far as Bethany, and lifting up his hands he blessed them. While he blessed them, he parted from them, and was carried up into heaven" (Lk 24:50–51, RSVCE). Likewise, in Acts he says, "As they were looking on, he was lifted up, and a cloud took him out of their sight" (Acts 1:9, RSVCE). These lines are serene and majestic, and they gather centuries of biblical expectation into one luminous fulfillment. Christ rises from the earth in blessing, and He ascends through the cloud of divine presence, and the disciples gaze upward with astonishment, because the One who was scourged, pierced, buried, and raised is now entering His royal session. Thus, the Ascension is the heavenly coronation of the victorious Son.

The language of enthronement has deep roots in Israel's Scriptures. Psalm 110 had already declared, "The Lord says to my lord:

'Sit at my right hand, till I make your enemies your footstool'" (Ps 110:1, RSVCE). This text became central for the apostolic preaching because it revealed the Messiah as David's Lord and the priestly king whose dominion comes from God Himself. Jesus applied this psalm to His own identity during His earthly ministry, and after the Resurrection the apostles proclaimed its fulfillment with boldness. St. Peter says at Pentecost, "Being therefore exalted at the right hand of God" and again, "For David did not ascend into the heavens; but he himself says, 'The Lord said to my Lord, Sit at my right hand'" (Acts 2:33–34, RSVCE). Therefore, the Ascension is the divine answer to Psalm 110, and Christ's heavenly session is the true throne from which all earthly history now receives its final meaning.

Likewise, Daniel had seen in prophetic vision "one like a son of man" who came "with the clouds of heaven" and was given "dominion and glory and kingdom, that all peoples, nations, and languages should serve him" (Dan 7:13–14, RSVCE). Jesus repeatedly called Himself the Son of Man, and in doing so He drew together humility, suffering, judgment, and glory into one messianic identity. At His trial before the high priest, He said, "You will see the Son of man seated at the right hand of Power, and coming with the clouds of heaven" (Mk 14:62, RSVCE). Therefore, the Ascension is the fulfillment of Daniel's vision. The cloud that receives Jesus is the sign of divine presence, the same biblical symbol that hovered over Sinai, filled the tabernacle, and overshadowed the holy mountain. Thus, Christ enters openly into the heavenly dominion foretold long before.

Where Jesus is Now

This matters deeply because the Ascension reveals where our Savior is now. He is risen, and He is reigning. He is alive, and He is enthroned. He is human forever, and He has brought human nature into heavenly glory. The Catechism teaches, "Christ's Ascension marks the definitive entrance of Jesus' humanity into God's heavenly domain" (CCC 665). That sentence should steady every anxious heart. Our humanity is already present before the Father in the person of the Son. The flesh He assumed from the Virgin has entered glory. The wounds of Calvary remain in the risen body that now shines in majesty. Therefore, heaven is forever marked by the humanity of Jesus Christ. The Incarnation reaches its royal consummation in the Ascension.

The Letter to the Hebrews gives this mystery extraordinary depth. It says, "We have a great high priest who has passed through the heavens, Jesus, the Son of God" (Heb 4:14, RSVCE). Again, "Christ has entered, not into a sanctuary made with hands, a copy of the true one, but into heaven itself, now to appear in the presence of God on our behalf" (Heb 9:24, RSVCE). Here the Ascension is revealed as a priestly entrance. Jesus ascends as eternal high priest who presents His redeeming work before the Father for us. The temple liturgy of Israel had always pointed beyond itself toward this heavenly reality. The high priest entered the Holy of Holies once a year with sacrificial blood on the Day of Atonement, and that sacred drama taught Israel that access to God required priesthood, sacrifice, holiness, and divine mercy. Yet Hebrews declares that all of this reached its fulfillment in Christ, who entered the true sanctuary through His own Blood and secured eternal redemption (Heb 9:11–12, RSVCE).

Therefore, the Ascension is covenantal at its core. The Son who shed the Blood of the New Covenant now presents the fruits of that redemption in the heavenly sanctuary and continuously intercedes for His people. Hebrews says, "He always lives to make intercession for them" (Heb 7:25, RSVCE). The Catechism echoes this beautifully: "Jesus Christ, the one priest of the new and eternal covenant, 'entered, not into a sanctuary made by human hands... but into heaven itself, now to appear in the presence of God on our behalf'" (CCC 662, quoting Heb 9:24). Consequently, the Ascension assures us that the Cross is eternally effective and the Resurrection eternally victorious and the covenant eternally alive in the person of the Son.

The Ascension Brings Joy

At this point one begins to see why the disciples could return from the Ascension "with great joy" (Lk 24:52, RSVCE). Human instinct might expect sorrow as the visible presence of Jesus had been withdrawn. Yet the apostles rejoice because they understand, at least in seed form, that His departure is for their good. He had already told them, "I go to prepare a place for you" (Jn 14:2, RSVCE), and again, "It is to your advantage that I go away" (Jn 16:7, RSVCE). The Ascension, therefore, is no loss of Christ. It is the expansion of His saving presence through heavenly lordship and the coming of the Holy Spirit. His bodily visibility is veiled from earthly sight, and yet His power, grace, and reign now reach His whole Church in a new way.

This opens a profoundly personal truth. The ascended Christ governs history even when earthly events seem chaotic and fragmented and bruising. Kings rise and fall. Cultures harden and dissolve. Institutions strengthen and weaken. Empires boast and then fade. Yet above every earthly tumult, Jesus Christ reigns at the Father's right hand. St. Paul says that God "raised him from the dead and made him sit at his right hand in the heavenly places, far above all rule and authority and power and dominion" (Eph 1:20–21, RSVCE). Again, he teaches that the Father "has delivered us from the dominion of darkness and transferred us to the kingdom of his beloved Son" (Col 1:13, RSVCE). Therefore, the Christian never lives beneath the final authority of Caesar, party, market, media, ideology, or fear. The Christian lives under the reign of the ascended Christ.

That kingship is neither abstract nor remote. The One enthroned in heaven remains the pierced Shepherd who knows His sheep by name. The One seated at the right hand is still the Bridegroom who loves His Church. The One invested with universal dominion is evermore the Lamb once slain. Revelation gathers these truths in radiant imagery when St. John beholds "a Lamb standing, as though it had been slain" in the heavenly throne room (Rev 5:6, RSVCE). The exalted Christ never ceases to be the crucified Christ. Consequently, when believers pray to the ascended Lord, they pray to One who reigns with scarred hands.

The Ascension Matters for Us Personally

The Catechism says, "Left to its own natural powers humanity does not have access to the 'Father's house,' to God's life and happiness. Only Christ can open to man such access" (CCC 661). This is why the Ascension matters for every soul. Our destiny is bound to His. Human life is forever altered because one of us, a true man united forever to true God, has entered the heavenly sanctuary. St. Leo the Great preached with splendid joy, "The ascension of Christ is our own exaltation" (*Sermon* 73.4). By this he meant that Christ's glorified humanity is the pledge of our own future participation in heavenly life. Since the Head has entered glory, the Body shall follow, the Bride journeys with hope, and the adopted children have a home prepared for them.

Accordingly, the Ascension shapes Christian hope in a uniquely royal and priestly way. Hope now looks upward without drifting into fantasy, because heaven has been opened by a historical person whose name is Jesus. Hope now rests in promise without dissolving into vague aspiration, because Christ Himself said, "And when I go and prepare a place for you, I will come again and will take you to myself" (Jn 14:3, RSVCE). The Catechism teaches that hope "responds to the aspiration to happiness which God has placed in the heart of every man" and it "keeps man from discouragement" and "opens up his heart in expectation of eternal beatitude" (CCC 1818). The Ascension strengthens this virtue by showing us the place toward which grace directs us.

It also transforms worship. The Church gathers to participate sacramentally in the heavenly liturgy of the enthroned Christ. Hebrews urges believers to draw near "to Mount Zion and to the city of the living God, the heavenly Jerusalem" (Heb 12:22, RSVCE). The Eucharistic liturgy, therefore, is never an isolated earthly ritual. It is participation in the worship of the ascended High Priest who unites heaven and earth. The Second Vatican Council teaches that in the liturgy "we take part in a foretaste of that heavenly liturgy which is celebrated in the holy city of Jerusalem" (*Sacrosanctum Concilium* 8). Thus, the Ascension means that Christian worship is lifted upward. The altar on earth is joined to the sanctuary above. The people of God worship under the headship of the enthroned Christ.

We Cannot Be Indifferent

This is why spiritual indifference becomes so dangerous. If Christ is ascended and enthroned, then time is charged with eternal significance. Our prayer reaches a living mediator. Our obedience reaches a living king. Our suffering reaches a living priest. Our sacraments reach a living Lord. St. Paul, therefore, says, "Set your minds on things that are above, where Christ is, seated at the right hand of God" (Col 3:1, RSVCE). That exhortation is neither sentimental nor vague. It means that earthly life must be ordered under heavenly truth. Ambition must be purified. Desire must be disciplined. Speech must be sanctified. Vocations must be lived under the gaze of the enthroned Son. Since Christ reigns, every compartment of life belongs to Him.

The Ascension also explains the Church's missionary urgency. Before ascending, Jesus says, "You shall receive power when the Holy Spirit has come upon you; and you shall be my witnesses" (Acts 1:8, RSVCE). Then in Matthew He declares, "All authority in heaven and on earth has been given to me. Go therefore and make disciples of all nations" (Mt 28:18–19, RSVCE). Mission flows from enthronement. Evangelization rises from kingship. The Church goes into the nations because Christ already reigns over the nations. She proclaims repentance and forgiveness because the crucified and risen Lord now possesses universal authority. Therefore, the Ascension produces apostolic courage. The disciples who once hid behind locked doors soon preach openly before rulers and councils because they know where Jesus is and who Jesus is.

Aristotle saw that man is political by nature and that the polis exists for the sake of the good life (*Politics*, I.2, 1252b27–30). Augustine later discerned that earthly cities are shaped by loves, either love of God unto self-forgetfulness or love of self unto contempt of God (*City of God*, XIV.28). The Ascension answers these concerns at their highest level, because the supreme political and moral truth of the universe is this: the true King has ascended. The highest common good is communion with God under Christ's reign. Every earthly order is, therefore, provisional and accountable. Civil life matters deeply. Yet no earthly power is absolute. The throne above judges every throne below.

St. Thomas Aquinas helps here as well. He teaches that Christ's Ascension is the cause of our salvation inasmuch as it prepares the way for us, raises our hope, and draws our hearts upward toward heavenly things (*Summa Theologiae*, III, q. 57, a. 1, ad 3; a. 6). In other words, the Ascension is medicinal for the soul. It lifts desire. It purifies longing. It teaches the heart where its treasure lies. The Christian who contemplates the ascended Christ learns gradually to measure life differently. Earthly success loses some of its seductive glow. Human praise becomes thinner. Hidden obedience becomes richer. Prayer becomes more confident. Suffering becomes more intelligible. Death becomes a passage under the lordship of the risen and ascended Lord.

We Look to Heaven

There is also a tender pastoral truth here. The disciples gazed upward until angels said, "Men of Galilee, why do you stand looking into heaven?" (Acts 1:11, RSVCE). The question is gentle and firm. Christ's ascension calls the Church upward, and then sends the Church outward. Contemplation and mission meet here. The believer must look to heaven, and then return to obedience on earth. One must adore the enthroned Christ, and then serve Him in ordinary duties, in hidden sacrifices, in works of mercy, in fidelity within vocation, in the courageous witness of word and life. The Ascension teaches active loyalty. Jesus is enthroned, and, therefore, His servants must labor in hope until He comes again.

Indeed, the angels continue, "This Jesus, who was taken up from you into heaven, will come in the same way as you saw him go into heaven" (Acts 1:11, RSVCE). Here the Ascension opens toward the Second Coming. The enthroned Christ is also the returning Christ. Therefore, the Church lives between Ascension and consummation. She lives by faith, nourished through sacraments, guided by the

Spirit, held in covenant communion, sustained by hope. The Catechism teaches that "since the Ascension God's plan has entered into its fulfillment. We are already at 'the last hour'" (CCC 670). That is a startling line. It means that Christian life unfolds in eschatological urgency. History has entered its decisive age. The King has taken His throne. The Spirit has been sent. The Gospel must go forth. The Church must endure. Souls must awaken.

Dear friend, this means your life is already taking place under the throne of the ascended Christ. He is not absent from your sufferings. He is not indifferent to your vocation. He is not distant from your prayers. He is not uninvolved in your battles with temptation, fatigue, grief, or discouragement. He intercedes for you. He reigns over you. He prepares a place for you. He sends grace to you. He calls you upward, and then sends you outward. Therefore, Christian life can never shrink into private sentiment or inherited identity or occasional religious memory. The enthroned Christ deserves the whole life.

The Ascension is the enthronement of the Son of Man foretold by Daniel, the fulfillment of the royal priesthood announced in Psalm 110, the heavenly entrance of the High Priest proclaimed in Hebrews, the exaltation of Christ's humanity into the Father's presence, the ground of the Church's mission, the source of sacramental confidence, the anchor of Christian hope, and the pledge of our future glory. Christ reigns now. His covenant mediation continues now. His blessing extends now. His authority governs now. His intercession sustains now. Therefore, the Christian soul must lift its eyes, order its loves, sanctify its days, and live courageously under the lordship of Jesus Christ, the crucified, risen, and ascended King.

Meditation Questions

1. Do I truly live as though Jesus Christ is reigning now at the right hand of the Father, or do I still allow earthly powers, anxieties, and passing troubles to govern my thoughts more than His kingship?
2. When I pray, do I remember that Christ "always lives to make intercession" for us (Heb. 7:25), and that my prayers rise through the living High Priest who has entered heaven on my behalf?
3. In what areas of my life have I grown too earthbound, too attached to comfort, success, recognition, control, or visible results?
4. What does it mean for me personally that Christ has taken human nature into heavenly glory, and that my humanity now has a place in the Father's house through Him?
5. Do I approach the Mass with the conviction that I am being drawn into the worship of the ascended Christ and the heavenly liturgy?
6. Have I allowed the Ascension to deepen my hope, especially in seasons of waiting, grief, disappointment, or spiritual fatigue?
7. Do I live as a witness of the enthroned Christ, or have I allowed fear, hesitation, or spiritual passivity to silence my faith?
8. In what specific ways do I still behave as though Christ were distant rather than present, reigning, interceding, and actively governing His Church?

9. How does the truth that Jesus will come again shape my use of time, my habits, my priorities, and my moral decisions?
10. What earthly concerns have grown too large in my imagination because I have not lifted my eyes often enough toward the throne of Christ?
11. Do I truly believe that no earthly ruler, ideology, cultural pressure, or personal failure has final authority over me, because I belong to the kingdom of the beloved Son (Col. 1:13)?
12. If Christ is enthroned now, what part of my life still resists His rule?

Spiritual Call to Action

This truth should lead the soul toward a more elevated Christian life, one marked by reverence, confidence, obedience, and mission under the lordship of the ascended Christ.

Therefore, over the next seven days, begin each day by lifting your eyes physically and spiritually upward and praying slowly: Lord Jesus Christ, ascended and enthroned, reign over my mind, my desires, my work, my speech, and my whole life today.

Then read one Ascension or heavenly kingship passage each day. Spend time with Luke 24:50–53, Acts 1:1–11, Psalm 110, Daniel 7:13–14, Hebrews 4:14–16, Hebrews 9:11–24, and Colossians 3:1–4. Read slowly. Read prayerfully. Ask the Lord to show you where your life has stayed too low, too distracted, or too shaped by earthly concerns.

Next, choose one concrete act of heavenly-minded discipline each day. Set aside unnecessary media for a fixed period. Pray the

Angelus or another brief prayer at midday. Pause before a crucifix or in church for adoration. Speak openly to one person about Christ. Reorder one habit that has kept your soul spiritually dull. Let each act say with your life that Christ reigns now.

Also, attend Mass this week with particular attention to the heavenly dimension of worship. Before Mass begins, consciously place your mind before the throne of Christ and say interiorly: Jesus, draw me into Your worship before the Father. Let me offer this liturgy with You and through You.

Then identify one area of discouragement in your life and bring it explicitly under Christ's kingship. Name it. Surrender it. Say aloud: Jesus Christ reigns above this. My future is under His lordship.

Finally, make one act of mission this week. Since the ascended Christ sends His Church into the world, do one deliberate thing that reflects that sending. Invite someone to Mass. Share a passage of Scripture. Encourage a fallen Catholic to return. Speak a word of truth with charity and courage. The enthroned Christ deserves witnesses, not spectators.

You may close each day with this prayer:

Lord Jesus Christ,
ascended into heaven and seated at the right hand of the Father,
You reign in glory and intercede for Your people.
Lift my heart toward heavenly things.
Free me from small ambitions and earthly distraction.
Teach me to pray with confidence, worship with reverence,
suffer with hope, and serve with courage.

Rule over every part of my life.
Prepare me for Your coming kingdom
and make me a faithful witness under Your holy reign.
Amen.

Chapter 4

Do Not Delay Responding

The crucifixion of Christ, the Resurrection of Christ, and the Ascension of Christ together place every human soul under an urgent summons, because once God has acted so decisively in His Son, delay in the spiritual life ceases to be a small weakness and becomes a serious danger to the heart, to the conscience, to the habits, to the will, and finally to the soul's relation with God Himself. Therefore, here, I speak genuinely. A delayed response to grace is dangerous. A postponed repentance is dangerous. A half-offered life is dangerous. A slow surrender is dangerous. The Gospel is too holy and the soul is too precious and death is too certain for us to live as though there will always be another season for obedience.

Scripture speaks with striking directness on this point. St. Paul writes, "Behold, now is the acceptable time; behold, now is the day of salvation" (2 Cor 6:2, RSVCE). That apostolic word comes with fire because it tears through the illusion that conversion may safely stay somewhere in the future. Likewise, the Letter to the Hebrews warns, "Today, when you hear his voice, do not harden your hearts" (Heb 3:7–8, RSVCE; cf. Ps 95:7–8, RSVCE). Notice the repeated emphasis on "today." Scripture confronts us with the holy urgency of grace. God speaks today. Grace is given today. The heart can harden today. Therefore, a response must also come today.

This urgency flows directly from the hour of Christ. The Son of God has already entered His hour through suffering, sacrifice, victory, and exaltation, hence the human person no longer lives in a vague religious landscape where ultimate things are distant and indistinct. The Lamb has been slain. The tomb is empty. The Son is enthroned. Heaven is open. The Spirit has been poured out. The Church has been born from the pierced side of Christ and sent into the nations. Consequently, history itself has entered its decisive age. The Catechism teaches, "Since the Ascension God's plan has entered into its fulfillment. We are already at 'the last hour'" (CCC 670). Friends, read that carefully. We are already in the last hour. This means that delay is not merely inefficient. It is spiritually perilous because it treats decisive grace as though it were indefinitely deferrable.

Delay Might Be Sinful

Moreover, sin itself thrives on delay. Few souls plunge suddenly into deep ruin without first learning the art of postponement. The conscience whispers. Grace stirs. Truth pierces. Yet the soul says, later, after this season, after this pleasure, after this ambition, after this indulgence, after this resentment, after this compromise, after this one more act of disobedience. In that way delay becomes the soft pillow of destruction. St. Augustine knew this inner warfare intimately when he wrote of his old prayer, "Grant me chastity and continence, but not yet" (*Confessions*, VIII.7.17). He desired God, and yet he still clung to delay. He longed for freedom, and yet he still negotiated with bondage. He wanted conversion, and yet he wanted time for the flesh. That divided heart is one of the oldest dramas in human life.

Accordingly, the danger of delay is not only that one stays where one is. The deeper danger is that habits deepen. Attachments tighten. Vision dims. Appetite grows more disordered. Shame grows more familiar. Resistance grows more practiced. Therefore, Scripture warns repeatedly against hardness of heart. Pharaoh hardened his heart before the Lord despite repeated signs and warnings (Ex 7–11, RSVCE). Israel in the wilderness hardened its heart despite deliverance from Egypt and divine provision in the desert (Ps 95:8–11, RSVCE). Zechariah says of rebellious people that "they made their hearts diamond-hard lest they should hear the law" (Zech 7:12, RSVCE). In all these cases delay gave way to hardening, and hardening gave way to judgment.

This should sober every Christian. The Catechism teaches that mortal sin, unless repented of, brings "exclusion from Christ's kingdom and the eternal death of hell" (CCC 1861). It also teaches that venial sin weakens charity, impedes progress in virtue, and disposes the soul toward graver sin (CCC 1863). Therefore, even what many call small indulgences matter deeply. A soul can grow dull gradually. The will can become sluggish gradually. Prayer can become thin gradually. Reverence can cool gradually. Spiritual drift rarely announces itself dramatically at first. It often begins through tolerated delay.

Repent Now

Our Lord Himself speaks with grave urgency in His preaching. "Repent, for the kingdom of heaven is at hand" (Mt 4:17, RSVCE). That declaration is immediate, direct, and pressing. The kingdom is at hand. Therefore, repentance cannot be shelved. Again Jesus says, "Strive to enter by the narrow door" (Lk 13:24, RSVCE). The word "strive" signifies exertion, earnestness, and decision. It calls for serious entry into the life of God. Likewise, Christ teaches, "Watch therefore, for you know neither the day nor the hour" (Mt 25:13, RSVCE). This comes at the end of the parable of the ten virgins, where five are wise and five are foolish, and the foolish discover too late that spiritual unreadiness cannot be remedied after the bridegroom has come (Mt 25:1–13, RSVCE). That parable is one of the clearest biblical warnings against delay. Preparation delayed becomes preparation denied.

Then there is the rich fool in Luke 12. He stores up goods for many years and says to himself, "Soul, you have ample goods laid up for many years; take your ease, eat, drink, be merry" (Lk 12:19, RSVCE). Yet God says to him, "Fool! This night your soul is required of you" (Lk 12:20, RSVCE). Here Christ cuts through perhaps the greatest illusion in fallen human life, namely the assumption of guaranteed future time. Delay feeds on presumed tomorrow. Yet tomorrow is never promised. Breath is a gift. Days are given. Life is fragile. "What is your life? For you are a mist that appears for a little time and then vanishes" (Jas 4:14, RSVCE). Therefore, to postpone obedience is to gamble with time that does not belong to us.

The Church has always taken this with utmost seriousness. Vatican II declares, "Since we know neither the day nor the hour, we should follow the advice of the Lord and watch constantly so that, when the single course of our earthly life is completed, we may merit to enter with Him into the marriage feast" (*Lumen Gentium* 48). Likewise, the Catechism says, "Death puts an end to human life as the time open to either accepting or rejecting the divine grace manifested in Christ" (CCC 1021). That is one of the most sober sentences in Catholic teaching. Death ends the time open to accepting or rejecting grace. Therefore, delay is dangerous because the season of response is finite. The soul is immortal. Earthly time is not.

Inner, Hidden Sins

Here we must also speak personally, because many believers imagine danger only in scandalous outward sins while ignoring the quieter interior forms of delay that damage the soul just as surely over time. A man delays prayer until his soul becomes unfamiliar with God. A woman delays forgiveness until bitterness becomes part of her speech and memory. A husband delays repentance for habitual lust until impurity colonizes his imagination. A wife delays charity until irritation shapes the atmosphere of the home. A priest delays deeper surrender until ministry becomes professional and thin. A young person delays vocational seriousness until pleasure becomes an unchallenged ruler. A lukewarm Catholic delays confession until shame and pride begin to guard the soul like armed sentries. In all these cases the danger is profound precisely because it can look externally manageable for a season.

Moreover, delay insults love. If Christ loved us unto death, rose for our justification, ascended for our glory, and now intercedes for us before the Father, then the proper response to such covenant love is a life offered in return with sincerity and eagerness. "We love, because he first loved us" (1 Jn 4:19, RSVCE). Delay says something disordered about love. It says that the heart still wants God, and yet also wants sin. It says that the conscience still recognizes truth, and yet prefers comfort. It says that the will still admires holiness, and yet clings to rival attachments. This is why divided love is dangerous. Christ says, "No servant can serve two masters" (Lk 16:13, RSVCE). A divided heart slowly becomes an unstable heart.

Aristotle teaches that moral life is formed by repeated acts, because virtue grows through habituation and vice, likewise, becomes rooted through repeated choices (*Nicomachean Ethics*, II.1, 1103a14–26). This means that delay is never empty time. One is always becoming someone. Each postponement forms the will. Each compromise shapes the character. Each act of surrender to appetite teaches the soul whom it obeys. St. Thomas Aquinas, drawing deeply from this moral vision and elevating it within Christian theology, teaches that habits incline powers toward certain acts and that repeated acts strengthen dispositions (*Summa Theologiae*, I-II, q. 49, a. 3; q. 51, a. 2). Therefore, if one delays holiness, one is not merely waiting. One is being formed away from it. Delay, then, is dangerous partly because it educates desire against God.

Blinding our Reason

At the same time, delay blinds the intellect. Sin darkens judgment. The Catechism teaches that through the Fall, man is subject to error and inclined toward evil in using his freedom (CCC 1739–1742). St. Paul speaks of Gentiles whose "senseless minds were darkened" (Rom 1:21, RSVCE). Again he warns that certain persons are "darkened in their understanding, alienated from the life of God because of the ignorance that is in them, due to their hardness of heart"

(Eph 4:18, RSVCE). Notice the sequence. Hardness of heart leads to darkened understanding. Moral resistance affects intellectual vision. Therefore, delay is not merely a weakness in execution. It gradually distorts perception itself. The soul begins by saying, later. Afterward it begins to say, perhaps this is not so serious. Then eventually it may say, perhaps this is not wrong at all. Delay can become doctrinal corruption through moral erosion.

This is one reason modern man is so vulnerable. We live amid technologies of distraction, habits of immediacy, endless entertainment, erotic saturation, perpetual noise, and a cultural atmosphere that constantly trains the will toward convenience and appetite. In such a world, delay feels natural. An age of distraction is, therefore, an age of spiritual danger.

Then there is the example of Felix in Acts 24. As Paul reasoned "about justice and self-control and future judgment, Felix was alarmed and said, 'Go away for the present; when I have an opportunity I will summon you'" (Acts 24:25, RSVCE). That sentence is one of the most haunting in the New Testament. Felix hears the truth. Felix is alarmed. Felix is morally pierced. Yet Felix delays. Scripture records no great conversion afterward. The reader is left with the terrible image of a man close to grace and yet unwilling to yield. Many souls live there. They are near enough to truth to be troubled and near enough to grace to be stirred, yet still unwilling to surrender today. The danger lies precisely there.

By contrast, Zacchaeus responds immediately. "Behold, Lord, the half of my goods I give to the poor" (Lk 19:8, RSVCE). The prodigal son says, "I will arise and go to my father" (Lk 15:18, RSVCE).

Matthew rises from the tax booth when called (Mt 9:9, RSVCE). Peter and Andrew leave their nets when summoned (Mt 4:20, RSVCE). The good thief cries out from the cross, "Jesus, remember me" (Lk 23:42, RSVCE). In each case grace elicits response. Imperfect souls still respond. Wounded souls still respond. Sinners still respond. The issue is not whether one comes with flawless strength. The issue is whether one yields when Christ calls.

Reject Despair

This is why despair must also be rejected. Some delay because they love sin. Others delay because they think themselves too ruined to return. Both are dangerous. Judas delayed repentance into destruction. Peter wept bitterly and returned through mercy (Mt 26:75; Jn 21:15–19, RSVCE). The difference is decisive. Christ's mercy is stronger than our past. The Catechism teaches, "There is no offense, however serious, that the Church cannot forgive" (CCC 982). Therefore, no reader should twist these truths into hopelessness. The warning is severe precisely because the mercy and love of God is so real.

Furthermore, the sacraments reveal how seriously God takes our response. Baptism gives new life. The Eucharist nourishes charity. Penance restores the fallen. Confirmation strengthens witness. Matrimony consecrates family life. Holy Orders configures men to Christ for service. Anointing strengthens the sick. These are not decorative religious options. They are covenant gifts through which Christ actively sanctifies His people. Therefore, to neglect sacramental life through delay is to refuse medicine while praising the physician. The Catechism says the Eucharist is "the source and summit of the Christian life" (CCC 1324). It teaches that individual and integral confession of grave sins are the ordinary means of reconciliation with God and the Church after baptism (CCC 1484). Delay from these gifts is dangerous because grace neglected leaves the soul weaker in the face of temptation.

So, what then should the soul do? First, tell the truth. Name the area of delay precisely. Vague remorse rarely produces conversion. Specific honesty does. Second, repent concretely. Christ died and rose to create repentant saints. Third, go to confession. Fourth, repair what can be repaired. Fifth, remove what feeds the delayed sin. Sixth, establish habits that teach the soul immediate obedience. Morning prayer. Scripture. Examination of conscience. Sunday Mass with reverence. Frequent confession. Eucharistic adoration. Spiritual reading. Acts of mercy. These are ordinary, and they are powerful. Holiness often begins through ordinary fidelity embraced immediately.

St. Benedict begins his Rule with a word of urgency: "Today if you hear his voice, harden not your hearts" (*Rule*, Prologue). St. Francis de Sales, likewise, urges prompt generosity toward God and warns against spiritual sluggishness in the devout life (*Introduction to the Devout Life*, Part I). These saints knew the human heart. Delay feels modest. In truth it is often a quiet revolt against surrender. By contrast, immediate obedience has a cleansing power. It weakens the lie that says holiness can wait. It teaches the will to move with grace. It retrains love.

Dear friend, there is a holy reason why this book has brought you from Cross to Resurrection to Ascension before arriving here. Once you have seen what Christ has done, delay becomes intolerable. The Cross says He loved you unto the end. The Resurrection says He conquered death for you. The Ascension says He reigns and intercedes for you now. Therefore, what exactly are you waiting for? Another collapse. Another humiliation. Another cycle of the same compromise. Another year of diminished prayer. Another layer of hardness over the heart. Another indulgence that further trains desire away from God. Delay has already cost too much.

The Lord says, "My son, give me your heart" (Prov 23:26, RSVCE). He asks for the whole heart. Now. "Seek the Lord while he may be found, call upon him while he is near" (Is 55:6, RSVCE). That prophetic line vibrates with mercy and urgency together. He is near. Therefore, seek Him. He is calling. Therefore, answer Him.

And so let this be said clearly. Do not delay responding. It is dangerous. Dangerous to the conscience. Dangerous to the will. Dangerous to prayer. Dangerous to love. Dangerous to your vocation. Dangerous to the habits that will shape your eternal future. Yet the danger is accompanied by hope, because the Christ who warns is the Christ who saves. The Christ who commands repentance is the Christ who shed His Blood for sinners. The Christ who sits on the throne is the Christ who still says, "Come to me" (Mt 11:28, RSVCE). Therefore, arise today. Return today. Confess today. Surrender today. Begin today. The hour of Christ has already come. Your hour to answer Him is now.

Meditation Questions

1. What area of my spiritual life have I been delaying most seriously, and why have I allowed that delay to remain?
2. When I hear the words, "Today, when you hear his voice, do not harden your hearts" (Heb. 3:7–8), what specific resistance in me is being exposed?
3. Have I mistaken delay for caution, wisdom, or emotional preparation when in truth it has become disobedience?
4. What sin, habit, attachment, resentment, indulgence, or spiritual compromise has grown stronger in me because I kept saying later?
5. Do I truly believe that time is a gift and that I am not promised endless opportunities for repentance?
6. In what ways has delay weakened my prayer, dulled my conscience, darkened my judgment, or reduced my capacity to love God fully?
7. Have I allowed shame to keep me from confession, or pride to keep me from honest repentance?
8. Where in my life have I heard grace calling clearly, yet continued to negotiate with God rather than surrender?
9. Am I living with the seriousness of one who knows that Christ has already died, risen, and ascended, and that history is already in its decisive hour?
10. Which biblical figure in this chapter resembles me most right now: Felix, Augustine before conversion, the foolish virgins, the rich fool, Zacchaeus, the prodigal son, or Peter?

11. What would immediate obedience to Christ look like for me in the next twenty-four hours?
12. If I were to die sooner than I expect, what unfinished repentance would I most grieve having delayed?

Spiritual Call to Action

We should end with a concrete decision. Our delay must be broken by concrete obedience.

Therefore, within the next twenty-four hours, do one thing you have been postponing in your spiritual life. Do not choose the easiest thing. Choose the truest thing. If you need confession, go. If you need to begin daily prayer again, begin today. If you need to remove a sinful habit, cut off its source today. If you need to reconcile with someone, take the first step today. If you need to return to Mass faithfully, resolve it now and prepare for it seriously.

Then, for the next seven days, begin each morning with this prayer: Lord Jesus Christ, I will not delay my response to You today. Give me courage for immediate obedience.

Also, read each day one passage that presses urgency upon the soul: Psalm 95, Isaiah 55:6–9, Matthew 25:1–13, Luke 12:13–21, Luke 13:22–30, Acts 24:24–27, and 2 Corinthians 6:1–10. Read slowly. Read prayerfully. Ask the Lord to show you how delay has worked in your heart.

Next, make a written list of three areas where you have been postponing obedience. Under each one, write one specific action you will take this week. Keep the actions concrete. No vague intentions. No spiritual poetry. Real obedience.

Then examine your use of time. For one full week, cut out one recurring distraction that weakens your vigilance and use that time for prayer, Scripture, silence, or spiritual reading. Let your schedule begin to reflect the seriousness of your soul.

If confession is needed, do not let this week end without going. Name your sins honestly. Receive absolution gratefully. Leave with a concrete amendment of life. If grave sin is involved, this should be your first action, not your last.

Finally, each evening make a brief examination of conscience and ask two questions only: Where did I delay God today? Where did I obey Him promptly? Let this train your heart toward readiness.

You may close each day with this prayer:

Lord Jesus Christ,
You entered Your hour for my salvation.
You loved me unto the end.
You rose in victory and reign in glory.
Save me from delay, from excuses, from compromise, and from spiritual laziness.
Break every resistance in me that keeps me from full surrender.
Give me an honest heart, a ready will, and a living love for You.
Teach me to answer Your grace today, while Your voice still calls me.
Amen.

Chapter 5

The Christian Life Cannot Be Casual

Once Christ has been crucified, raised, and ascended, the Christian life can never again be treated as a mild religious attachment added onto an otherwise self-directed existence, because the Gospel is not a decorative truth for private comfort and the Church is not a cultural accessory and grace is not a spiritual fragrance laid lightly upon an unchanged soul. Rather, Christ has entered history decisively and covenantally, and through His Blood He has claimed a people for the Father, and through His Resurrection He has opened new life, and through His Ascension He now reigns and intercedes. Therefore, a casual Christianity is a contradiction. It misunderstands the Cross, diminishes the Resurrection, forgets the throne, and hollows out discipleship until only habit and vocabulary remain.

This must be said sincerely because many souls sincerely call Jesus Lord while still arranging life around comfort, distraction, convenience, appetite, ambition, and social respectability. That condition is spiritually dangerous precisely because it can preserve outward religious form while the interior life grows increasingly thin. Our Lord speaks directly into such conditions when He says, "Why do you call me 'Lord, Lord,' and not do what I tell you?" (Lk 6:46, RSVCE). That question cuts through every sentimental profession that lacks obedient substance. Christ rejects confessions that are severed from covenant fidelity. To call Him Lord is to belong to Him. To belong to Him is to obey Him. To obey Him is to order the whole life under His kingship.

Do Not Be Lukewarm

Moreover, Jesus warns the Church in Laodicea with severe tenderness, "Because you are lukewarm, and neither cold nor hot, I will spew you out of my mouth" (Rev 3:16, RSVCE). The language shocks because lukewarmness is often socially acceptable and religiously manageable. It looks tame. It looks civilized. It looks moderate. Yet the risen Christ speaks of it with disgust. Why? Because lukewarmness gives Him a divided heart, a measured loyalty, a restrained obedience, and a partial surrender. It offers Him recognition without fire, ritual without hunger, speech without sacrifice, identity without transformation. Therefore, the Christian life cannot be casual because Christ Himself refuses to treat it casually.

This begins with the nature of covenant. A covenant is never a loose arrangement of mutual goodwill. In Scripture it is sacred, binding, solemn, relational, and ordered toward communion through oath, loyalty, sacrifice, and fidelity. At Sinai the Lord bound Israel to Himself as His treasured possession among the nations (Ex 19:5, RSVCE). Moses sealed that covenant in blood and declared, "Behold the blood of the covenant which the Lord has made with you" (Ex 24:8, RSVCE). Likewise, Christ, in instituting the Eucharist, says, "This is my blood of the covenant, which is poured out for many" (Mk 14:24, RSVCE). Therefore, if Christians live under the New Covenant in the Blood of the Son, then their life with God is not casual by definition. It is a blood-bought belonging. It is sacrificial communion. It is consecrated life.

The Catechism reinforces this with great force. "The whole Christian life bears the mark of the spousal love of Christ and the

Church" (CCC 1617). Again, "Baptism not only purifies from all sins, but also makes the neophyte 'a new creature,' an adopted son of God, who has become a 'partaker of the divine nature,' member of Christ and coheir with him, and a temple of the Holy Spirit" (CCC 1265). These are staggering realities. A baptized Christian is not merely someone with improved beliefs. He is a new creature. He belongs to Christ. He participates in divine life through grace. He has been consecrated. Consequently, casual living after baptism is not simply disappointing. It is a failure to live according to what one has become.

St. Paul presses this truth relentlessly. "You are not your own; you were bought with a price. So glorify God in your body" (1 Cor 6:19–20, RSVCE). Notice how direct this is. The Christian is not his own. The Christian has been bought. The Christian, therefore, owes God embodied obedience. Paul is addressing sexual immorality there, yet the principle reaches the whole of life. Time is not one's own. Speech is not one's own. Desire is not one's own. Money is not one's own. Gifts are not one's own. Family life is not one's own. Vocation is not one's own. The Christian lives as one redeemed and claimed. Therefore, any version of faith that leaves the basic structure of self-possession intact has failed to receive the apostolic Gospel at its depth.

Participate in Christ's Life

Furthermore, the Christian life involves participation in the very life of Christ. "It is no longer I who live, but Christ who lives in me" (Gal 2:20, RSVCE). St. Paul speaks of an actual participation through grace in the living Christ. The Catechism says, "Grace is a participation in the life of God" (CCC 1997). Therefore, casual Christianity is inadequate because grace itself is far too profound for superficial living. Divine life has entered the soul. The Holy Spirit dwells within. Christ nourishes His people in the Eucharist. The Father adopts and draws them. How then can the response be thin, distracted, and unformed?

This is why Our Lord speaks in such absolute terms about discipleship. "If any man would come after me, let him deny himself and take up his cross daily and follow me" (Lk 9:23, RSVCE). Also, "He who loves father or mother more than me is not worthy of me" (Mt 10:37, RSVCE). Again, "Whoever of you does not renounce all that he has cannot be my disciple" (Lk 14:33, RSVCE). These sayings are not rhetorical exaggerations designed merely to stir religious emotion. They reveal the structure of discipleship. Christ claims primacy over every natural attachment and every earthly possession. He orders all relationships beneath His lordship. Therefore, casual Christianity fails because it rejects Christ as the center of everything.

The Church has always taught this. Vatican II says, "All the faithful of Christ of whatever rank or status are called to the fullness of the Christian life and to the perfection of charity" (*Lumen Gentium* 40). That sentence dismantles the convenient fiction that serious holiness belongs only to monks, nuns, priests, theologians, mystics, or visibly heroic souls. All the faithful are called to fullness. All the faithful are called to charity perfected through grace. Holiness is not an elective track within Catholicism. It is the normal end of Christian life. Therefore, casual living is incompatible with the universal call to holiness. One may be weak, wounded, and still growing. One may struggle severely. Yet one cannot make peace with mediocrity as though it were the ordinary ideal.

This point becomes even sharper when one considers the Eucharist. Christ says, "He who eats my flesh and drinks my blood has eternal life" (Jn 6:54, RSVCE). The Catechism teaches that the Eucharist is "the source and summit of the Christian life" (CCC 1324). If that is true, then Christian existence is ordered around sacramental communion with the crucified and risen Lord Himself. A casual approach to Mass, therefore, betrays a disorder of love. The altar is the place of covenant renewal and sacrificial communion. It is where the Church receives the Body and Blood of the Lord. It is where heaven bends toward earth through liturgy. Accordingly, one cannot live casually while approaching such holy fire. St. Paul warns, "Whoever, therefore, eats the bread or drinks the cup of the Lord in an unworthy manner will be guilty of profaning the body and blood of the Lord" (1 Cor 11:27, RSVCE). This is serious language because the Eucharist is serious glory.

Likewise, the sacrament of Penance exposes the absurdity of casual Christianity. If Christ shed His Blood for the remission of sins, and if He entrusted to the apostles the ministry of forgiveness, saying, "If you forgive the sins of any, they are forgiven" (Jn 20:23, RSVCE), then the Christian who drifts for long seasons from confession lives beneath the privileges of redemption. The Catechism says, "Those who approach the sacrament of Penance obtain pardon from God's mercy for the offense committed against him" (CCC 1422). Therefore, confession is not a gloomy burden imposed upon religious people. It is covenant mercy made available through

Christ. Casual Christianity delays confession, minimizes sin, rationalizes compromise, and slowly forgets the sweetness of absolution. Serious Christianity returns again and again to the fountain of mercy.

Christian Love

At this point one must also speak of love, because Christianity is a life of covenant love. Yet love itself proves why casualness is impossible. No husband worthy of the name would tell his bride that he loves her casually. No devoted mother would speak of her child with detached moderation. No true friend would boast of half-hearted fidelity. Love by its own nature reaches toward totality. It wants union, gift, nearness, delight, sacrifice, and perseverance. Thus, when Jesus says, "You shall love the Lord your God with all your heart, and with all your soul, and with all your mind" (Mt 22:37, RSVCE), He is revealing the true shape of created life. Casual Christianity is, therefore, also a failure of love. It offers God fragments instead of wholeness.

St. Augustine saw this with piercing insight when he wrote, "You have made us for yourself, and our heart is restless until it rests in you" (*Confessions*, I.1.1). Restlessness is the human condition under misdirected love. The heart seeks repose in lesser goods, partial pleasures, career success, erotic gratification, admiration, entertainment, intellectual vanity, political excitement, or family idolization, and yet the heart is inwardly unsettled because it was created for God. Casual Christianity attempts to solve that restlessness by giving God a place among other loves rather than above them and through them. Augustine shows why that cannot work. The heart must rest in God, not merely visit Him.

Ongoing Growth

This also means that the Christian life requires formation. It cannot survive on occasional inspiration. Virtue must be built. Prayer must be disciplined. Conscience must be educated. Desire must be purified. Scripture must be ingested deeply. The mind must be renewed. St. Paul says, "Be transformed by the renewal of your mind" (Rom 12:2, RSVCE). He also tells Timothy, "Train yourself in godliness" (1 Tim 4:7, RSVCE). The word train is crucial. One trains because a holy life is one that cooperates with divine grace. The Catechism teaches that the moral virtues are acquired by education, deliberate acts, and perseverance in repeated effort (CCC 1839). Therefore, casual Christianity is too untrained to endure. It wants the fruits of sanctity without the disciplines through which grace forms the soul.

Aristotle can help illuminate this structure. He teaches that we become just by doing just acts and temperate by doing temperate acts (*Nicomachean Ethics*, II.1, 1103a31–1103b2). Christian theology receives this moral insight and elevates it within grace. St. Thomas Aquinas explains that human acts form habits and that habits incline powers toward certain acts (*Summa Theologiae*, I-II, q. 49, a. 3; q. 50, a. 5). Therefore, the Christian who prays regularly becomes increasingly fitted for prayer. The Christian who confesses seriously becomes more truthful inwardly. The Christian who practices chastity becomes more integrated in desire. The Christian who gives generously becomes freer from greed. By contrast, casual Christianity trains the opposite habits. It trains irregularity, spiritual forgetfulness, soft will, indulgent appetite, and selective obedience.

Modern culture deepens this danger. We inhabit an age that catechizes people into distraction, constant novelty, shallow reaction, self-display, sexual confusion, digital dependency, and immediate gratification. In such an atmosphere, casual Christianity can flourish outwardly because it asks little and conforms easily. It requires no serious fasting, no sustained silence, no sacrificial generosity, no stable prayer, no doctrinal depth, no disciplined imagination, no real custody of the senses. Yet Christ died to create saints. Thus, a culture of distraction and a Gospel of crucified love cannot be reconciled through casual religious habits.

Be Vigilant

This is why the New Testament repeatedly calls believers to vigilance. "Be sober, be watchful. Your adversary the devil prowls around like a roaring lion" (1 Pet 5:8, RSVCE). "Work out your own salvation with fear and trembling" (Phil 2:12, RSVCE). "Let us lay aside every weight, and sin which clings so closely" (Heb 12:1, RSVCE). Such exhortations do not imply nervous insecurity about God's goodness. Rather, they reveal the seriousness of spiritual warfare and the necessity of alert cooperation with grace. The Catechism teaches that the Christian life is engaged in a battle and that the drama of this world passes through "a hard battle against the powers of darkness" (CCC 409). Therefore, a casual Christian is like a sleeping sentry. He may still wear the uniform. He may still speak the right language. Yet he is unfit for the battle in which he already finds himself.

Furthermore, Christian vocation itself proves that casualness is impossible. Marriage is not casual. Parenthood is not casual. Priesthood is not casual. Religious life is not casual. The single life lived for the kingdom is not casual. Each state of life is a covenant form of discipleship in which Christ sanctifies a soul through real duties, real sacrifices, real loves, and real obediences. Husbands are told to love their wives "as Christ loved the church and gave himself up for her" (Eph 5:25, RSVCE). Parents must bring up children "in the discipline and instruction of the Lord" (Eph 6:4, RSVCE). Priests are stewards of mysteries and shepherds of souls. Consecrated persons embody radical eschatological witness. Therefore, a casual Christianity empties the vocation of its supernatural seriousness and leaves people spiritually underprepared for the very life they are called to live.

The saints show another way. St. Ignatius of Antioch desired to belong wholly to Christ and wrote with burning love of union with Him through suffering and fidelity (*Letter to the Romans*). St. Teresa of Avila insisted that mental prayer and friendship with Christ must be pursued earnestly and perseveringly (*Life*, VIII.5). St. John Paul II preached that Christianity cannot be reduced to "a vague religiosity" and called believers to "a training in holiness" (*Novo Millennio Ineunte* 30–31). These voices differ in temperament and era, yet they agree in substance. The Christian life is total. It is demanding. It is beautiful. It is grace-filled. It is serious. No saint ever became holy casually.

Be Sincere

Yet the Church is not calling for scrupulosity, theatrical intensity, or joyless strain. The Christian life cannot be casual, and, likewise, it cannot be false. It is deeply human. It includes fatigue, recovery, laughter, friendship, meals, beauty, rest, work, and ordinary domestic life. Christ Himself ate with friends, attended feasts, withdrew for prayer, and blessed children. The point is not that every hour must feel emotionally dramatic. The point is that every dimension of life must belong to God. Serious Christianity is not permanent intensity. It is a stable consecration. It is a whole life placed under Christ's lordship through love and discipline and sacramental grace.

This is where the deeply personal character of discipleship returns. Each soul must ask with honesty, what in me still treats faith as background rather than center. Where have I become selective with Christ? Where do I gladly receive consolation and yet withhold surrender. Where do I preserve respectable religious identity and yet resist costly obedience? These questions matter because casualness often hides beneath familiar forms. One attends Mass, yet without hunger. One prays, yet without attentiveness. One reads Scripture, yet without readiness to obey. One speaks of God, yet without deep interior surrender. Therefore, the remedy begins with truthfulness before God.

Then comes the response. Christ poured out His Blood. He conquered death, and took His seat at the Father's right hand as priest and king. Therefore, the fitting Christian response is a life ordered in reverent seriousness and joyful fidelity. All aspects of our life, relationships, prayer, sacraments, work, etc. All must be conformed to Christ fully. This is simply Christian life lived according to what it is.

The Catechism says, "The dignity of man rests above all on the fact that he is called to communion with God" (CCC 27). If that is our dignity, then casual Christianity is beneath our calling. We were made for communion, redeemed for communion, fed for communion, disciplined for communion, and destined for communion. Therefore, let none of us settle for a thin version of faith that leaves the heart unformed and the will only partially yielded. Christ deserves our whole life. He deserves the first thought in the morning, the guarded imagination, the examined conscience, the faithful body, the disciplined tongue, the generous hand, the ordered household, the sacrificial vocation, the kneeling soul.

And so the Church says what the Gospel says in its own way. The Christian life cannot be casual. It is a covenant life. It is a cruciform life. It is a resurrection life. It is Eucharistic life. It is ecclesial life. It is Spirit-filled life under the throne of the ascended Christ. Therefore, live awake. Live reverently. Live sacramentally. Live obediently. Live with love that has been purified through truth and disciplined through grace. Christ died and rose so that you might belong to Him entirely.

Meditation Questions

1. In what ways have I allowed my Christian life to become casual, habitual, distracted, or merely external?

2. Do I truly live as one who has been "bought with a price" (1 Cor. 6:20), or do I still behave as though my life belongs chiefly to me?
3. Have I treated prayer as essential communion with God, or as something optional to fit around convenience?
4. What does my actual use of time reveal about the seriousness or casualness of my discipleship?
5. Do I approach Sunday Mass and the Holy Eucharist with reverence, hunger, and preparation, or with routine and inward detachment?
6. Have I allowed confession to become infrequent because of shame, laziness, pride, or spiritual dullness?
7. In what areas of my life have I offered Christ religious language while still resisting costly obedience?
8. Do I love the Lord with my whole heart, soul, and mind, or have I given Him only the safer and easier parts of myself?
9. What habits in me are forming a more disciplined saintly life, and what habits are forming a thinner and softer soul?
10. How has modern distraction weakened my attention to God, my custody of the senses, and my seriousness about holiness?
11. Am I pursuing the universal call to holiness as something meant truly for me, or have I quietly assumed that deeper sanctity belongs to other people?
12. If someone examined my daily life closely, would they see evidence that Christ is truly the center of it?

Spiritual Call to Action

These truths should lead to a deliberate reordering of life. Casual Christianity is broken by concrete fidelity.

Therefore, for the next seven days, begin each morning with this prayer: Lord Jesus Christ, You did not give Yourself for me casually. Teach me to live for You seriously, lovingly, and wholly today.

Then choose three non-negotiable daily acts for this week and keep them faithfully. Let them be simple and firm. For example, fifteen minutes of prayer, one passage of Scripture read slowly, and one nightly examination of conscience. Do not choose impressive things. Choose faithful things. Let stability begin to retrain the soul.

Next, examine your week honestly in five areas: prayer, Sunday worship, confession, use of time, and purity of heart. Write down where casualness has entered. Name it. Vague regret will accomplish very little. Honest naming begins real change.

Then make one concrete act of reverence toward the Eucharist this week. Attend Mass with greater preparation. Arrive early. Kneel and recollect yourself. Read the readings beforehand. Make a deliberate thanksgiving afterward. Let your worship reflect the holiness of the One you receive.

Also, remove one habitual distraction that has made your spiritual life thinner. It may be unnecessary scrolling, idle media, background noise, or some recurring indulgence that weakens recollection. Replace that time with prayer, silence, spiritual reading, or a walk with God.

If you have delayed confession, make it a priority this week. Do not let casualness stay protected by postponement. Bring your sins truthfully to Christ in the sacrament and receive His mercy with gratitude and firm purpose.

Finally, choose one area of vocation where your response has become passive, shallow, or irregular, whether in marriage, family life, work, friendship, chastity, charity, or witness. Take one concrete step this week that says with your actions: Jesus Christ is Lord here too.

You may close each day with this prayer:

Lord Jesus Christ,
You shed Your Blood to make me Your own.
Save me from lukewarmness, from distraction, and from half-hearted religion.
Teach me to pray with attention,
to worship with reverence,
to repent with honesty,
and to obey with love.
Take every part of my life under Your lordship
and make me faithful in the ordinary things
through which saints are formed. Amen.

Chapter 6

Suffering, Holiness, and Mission

Suffering is part of every human life, and when it enters, it reaches far beyond bodily pain or visible loss; it touches memory, hope, family, work, prayer, endurance, and one's deepest understanding of God, of self, and of the purpose of earthly life, and, therefore, no serious Christian vision can treat suffering as a side issue or as a temporary interruption in an otherwise smooth pilgrimage, because the Lord Jesus Christ chose to redeem the world through sacrificial love, and by that divine choice He joined suffering, holiness, and mission in a way that forever changes how the disciple must understand his own path in this fallen world.

From the beginning of Scripture, suffering is bound up with the rupture of sin and with the long ache of exile from Eden, for after the rebellion of our first parents the earth yields thorns, labor grows painful, relationships fracture, and death enters history with all its bitterness and sorrow (Gen 3:16–19, RSVCE), and yet even there the Lord gives a promise, since the seed of the woman shall crush the serpent though the heel is struck in the conflict (Gen 3:15, RSVCE), and already in that first gospel the biblical imagination begins to see that redemption will come to finally save us from all of it.

The History of Israel

Accordingly Israel's history becomes a long school of redemptive trial, because Abraham leaves homeland and kindred and learns to trust through waiting, wandering, and costly obedience (Gen 12:1–4; 22:1–18, RSVCE), Joseph descends into betrayal, slavery, false accusation, and prison before providence raises him for the saving of many lives (Gen 50:20, RSVCE), Moses bears the burden of a stubborn people in the wilderness, David suffers pursuit and humiliation before kingship, the prophets endure rejection and loneliness, and the psalms repeatedly give voice to the righteous sufferer who cries from affliction and yet still cleaves to the Lord. "The Lord is near to the brokenhearted" (Ps 34:18, RSVCE). "It is good for me that I was afflicted, that I might learn thy statutes" (Ps 119:71, RSVCE). God forms His servants through endurance, and through that endurance He makes them instruments for others.

This pattern reaches its blazing fulfillment in Christ. Isaiah saw Him in advance as the Servant who would be "despised and rejected by men; a man of sorrows, and acquainted with grief" and who would bear our griefs and carry our sorrows, though the prophet also says that "upon him was the chastisement that made us whole" (Is 53:3–5, RSVCE). Here the Old Covenant expectation deepens toward a mystery that fully comes into view only in Jesus, namely that suffering taken up in obedient covenant love becomes the pathway through which salvation reaches the many. Therefore, when the Son of God takes flesh, He enters as the Lamb and suffering Messiah whose hour moves steadily toward Calvary.

Our Lord makes this plain. "If any man would come after me, let him deny himself and take up his cross daily and follow me" (Lk 9:23, RSVCE). That summons is direct and piercing. It calls for embodied participation. It calls for a life shaped by the same pattern that shaped the Master. Then again, after the Resurrection, Jesus says to the disciples on the road to Emmaus, "Was it not necessary that the Christ should suffer these things and enter into his glory?" (Lk 24:26, RSVCE). Glory and suffering are thus joined in the divine economy. The path of the Christ becomes the path of the Christian. Therefore, suffering in the Christian life is never a meaningless leftover from a broken universe alone. Through union with Christ, it becomes a place of communion, purification, and apostolic fruitfulness.

The Cross

The Catechism speaks with luminous depth here: "The cross is the unique sacrifice of Christ, the 'one mediator between God and men.' But because in his incarnate divine person he has in some way united himself to every man, 'the possibility of being made partners, in a way known to God, in the paschal mystery' is offered to all men" (CCC 618). That sentence gives the whole chapter its theological center. Christ's suffering is unique, sufficient, and unrepeatable as redemption. Yet through grace the disciple is drawn into living participation in that Paschal mystery.

St. Paul gives perhaps the most concentrated expression of this mystery when he writes, "I rejoice in my sufferings for your sake, and in my flesh I complete what is lacking in Christ's afflictions for the sake of his body, that is, the church" (Col 1:24, RSVCE). Nothing is lacking in the redemptive power of Christ's Passion. The lack is in our participation. The Head has suffered once for all. The members are still being configured to Him through history. Therefore, Paul can rejoice, because his tribulations, united to Jesus, become fruitful for the Church. Here suffering, holiness, and mission are inseparable. His pain sanctifies him through deeper conformity to Christ, and that sanctification becomes service for the Body.

This is why holiness can never be separated from the cross. Vatican II teaches, "The classes and duties of life are many, yet holiness is one, that sanctity which is cultivated by all who are moved by the Spirit of God" and then speaks of those who follow "the poor Christ, the humble and cross-bearing Christ" (*Lumen Gentium* 41). Again, the Council says that martyrdom is the supreme gift and "proof of love" and then adds that all the faithful must be prepared to confess Christ before men and to follow Him on the way of the cross (*Lumen Gentium* 42). In other words, holiness is Christlikeness, covenant fidelity proven through sacrifice.

The Saints and Suffering

Moreover, the saints teach the same lesson. St. Ignatius of Antioch, on his way to martyrdom, desired to belong wholly to Christ and wrote, "Let me be food for the wild beasts" so that he might attain to the Lord (*Letter to the Romans* 4). St. Teresa of Avila, writing from the school of prayer, saw trial as one of the means by which the Lord purifies and strengthens the soul for deeper union (*Life* 11.10). St. John Paul II, in his apostolic letter on Christian suffering, wrote that suffering is present "in order to unleash love" (*Salvifici Doloris* 30). That phrase is extraordinarily important. In Christ, suffering can release love from the prison of self-concern and direct it toward God and neighbor with greater purity and freedom.

This mystery also reasonably makes sense when one remembers that human excellence is forged through acts, endurance, and rightly ordered love. Aristotle teaches that virtue is formed through habituation and that courage is perfected in facing what is difficult for the sake of the noble (*Nicomachean Ethics* II.1, III.6–9). Christian revelation receives this insight and raises it into a far greater horizon, because the noble end is now seen in the light of Christ crucified and risen. St. Thomas Aquinas, therefore, teaches that patience preserves the good of reason against sorrow, and fortitude strengthens the will amid grave trials (*Summa Theologiae* II-II, q. 136, a. 1; q. 123, a. 2). Grace heals and elevates nature. Thus, suffering becomes a school where patience, fortitude, hope, humility, and charity may be trained under the hand of God.

Still, such truths must never become cold formulas. Suffering is deeply personal. It reaches the husband watching his wife decline in sickness. It reaches the mother grieving a child. It reaches the priest who labors with hidden loneliness. In such places, merely conceptual answers are thin. The Christian needs Christ Himself. He needs the One who wept at Lazarus's tomb (Jn 11:35, RSVCE), who cried in Gethsemane, "My soul is very sorrowful, even to death" (Mt 26:38, RSVCE), who learned obedience through what He suffered (Heb 5:8, RSVCE), and who from the Cross entrusted His spirit to the Father (Lk 23:46, RSVCE). The Christian suffers with a Savior who knows anguish from within.

Therefore, the first task of the suffering disciple is union. "Abide in me, and I in you" (Jn 15:4, RSVCE). Suffering without union can sour into resentment or despair. Suffering within union can become sanctifying. The difference lies in whether the soul clings to Christ and offers the trial with Him and in Him. The Catechism says, "By his passion and death on the cross Christ has given a new meaning to suffering: it can henceforth configure us to him and unite us with his redemptive Passion" (CCC 1505). That new meaning transforms its spiritual horizon. The trial may be severe. Tears may remain. Yet the soul begins to say: Lord, use this. Lord, join this to Your Cross. Lord, let this purify me. Lord, let this serve Your Church.

Union with God Produces Holiness

Such a union gradually produces holiness. Holiness often grows through hidden endurance. A soul may become more detached from earthly vanities through one deep sorrow than through many comfortable sermons. Prayer may become more sincere when stripped of emotional sweetness. Love may become more mature when it must persevere without recognition. St. Peter writes, "Now for a little while you may have to suffer various trials, so that the genuineness of your faith, more precious than gold which though perishable is tested by fire, may redound to praise and glory and honor at the revelation of Jesus Christ" (1 Pet 1:6–7, RSVCE).

This is one reason why a life of mission so often grows from wounded places. Those who have suffered with Christ can speak of Him with a certain authority of soul. They know the difference between slogans and hope. They know what mercy means. They know how fragile human strength is. They know how sustaining grace can be. St. Paul says that God "comforts us in all our affliction, so that we may be able to comfort those who are in any affliction" (2 Cor 1:4, RSVCE). Here again suffering, holiness, and mission converge. Affliction received in Christ becomes a ministry to others. The Christian who has been consoled by God becomes capable of consoling. The Christian who has been sustained becomes capable of strengthening. The Christian who has endured becomes capable of teaching endurance with credibility.

Accordingly, mission is not only what happens on platforms or in pulpits or through dramatic apostolic enterprises. Mission also happens in the ordinary circumstances of human life, and unadvertised sacrifices offered in union with Jesus for the salvation of souls. A bedridden saint may do more for the Church than many highly visible workers. A mother offering her exhaustion to God with faith may become a missionary in her household more profoundly than she realizes. A father bearing financial pressure with prayerful integrity may preach Christ powerfully through steadfast love. A priest carrying hidden sorrow while faithfully celebrating Mass may nourish countless souls from the altar. Thus, the age's obsession with visible impact must yield to the Gospel's deeper law of fruitfulness through the Cross.

Our Lord Himself teaches this law: "Unless a grain of wheat falls into the earth and dies, it remains alone; but if it dies, it bears much fruit" (Jn 12:24, RSVCE). Mission in the Christian sense is always cruciform. It always includes dying to self, to vanity, to control, to comfort, to self-display, to impatience, to the demand that one's service be immediately fruitful in visible terms. The missionary soul learns to sow in tears. "He that goes forth weeping, bearing the seed for sowing, shall come home with shouts of joy" (Ps 126:6, RSVCE). Such lines reveal a law of covenant fruitfulness. God often hides the harvest while forming the sower.

This matters profoundly in our urgent age. Yet Jesus says, "Every branch that does bear fruit he prunes, that it may bear more fruit" (Jn 15:2, RSVCE). Pruning hurts. It cuts away excess. It removes illusions. It exposes dependence. Still, through such divine surgery the soul becomes more fruitful. Hence a mission without sanctification becomes dangerous. It may produce noise. It may produce attention. It will not produce lasting spiritual fruit of the kind Christ desires. Therefore, the disciple must accept that the Lord prunes those He means to use deeply.

The Sacraments and Suffering

The Church's sacramental life sustains this mystery. In Baptism we are plunged into Christ's death and Resurrection (Rom 6:3–4, RSVCE). In the Eucharist the sacrifice of Calvary is made present sacramentally and the faithful receive the Body and Blood of the Lord, source and summit of Christian life (CCC 1324). In Penance the wounded sinner returns and is healed by mercy (CCC 1422). In the Anointing of the Sick the Church entrusts the suffering believer to the Lord and asks for grace, strength, and salvation (CCC 1520–1523). Consequently, suffering in Catholic life is never isolated from worship. It is gathered into liturgy and often transformed through sacramental grace into a divine offering.

Mary reveals this beautifully. Simeon told her, "A sword will pierce through your own soul also" (Lk 2:35, RSVCE). At Calvary she stayed with the Son in sorrowful fidelity (Jn 19:25–27, RSVCE). Vatican II says that she "faithfully persevered in her union with her Son unto the cross" (*Lumen Gentium* 58). Her suffering was not sterile grief. It was maternal participation in the redemptive work of Christ through obedient love. Therefore, she becomes for the Church a model of how to suffer with faith, for from the Cross she receives a new motherhood in the beloved disciple.

Every one of us must eventually ask what he is doing with suffering now. One may waste it through bitterness. One may numb it through distractions. One may turn it inward through self-pity. Or one may bring it to Christ and say, Lord, unite this to Your Passion. Sanctify me through it. Use it for Your Church. Save souls through it. That prayer changes the interior stance of the soul. It turns pain toward love. It turns trial toward offering. It turns endurance toward mission. Such a prayer makes one eucharistic. It makes one capable of being offered.

This is why St. Paul can say, "We are afflicted in every way, but not crushed; perplexed, but not driven to despair" and then explain that he is "always carrying in the body the death of Jesus, so that the life of Jesus may also be manifested" (2 Cor 4:8–10, RSVCE). There, in one passage, the whole chapter comes to expression. The death of Jesus carried in the body becomes the manifestation of the life of Jesus. The apostolic life is marked by wounds and resurrectional power together. Therefore, suffering is not the enemy of mission in the Christian vocation. Very often it is the furnace in which the mission is made fruitful.

Martyrdom

The Catechism also teaches that martyrdom is the supreme witness given to the truth of the faith and means bearing witness even unto death (CCC 2473). While few are called to bloody martyrdom, every disciple is called to a daily white martyrdom of self-gift, renunciation, endurance, and covenant loyalty. The Christian husband dies to his selfishness for the sake of his bride. The Christian wife dies to resentment and perseveres in love. The Christian parent dies to convenience for the formation of children. The priest dies to private ownership of his life. The consecrated religious dies to worldly possession and self-direction. In each case, holiness grows through sacrifice, and mission flows from holiness.

And so suffering, holiness, and mission belong together because Christ has joined them in Himself. He suffered and thereby revealed perfect filial obedience and covenant love. Through that suffering He sanctified human suffering and made it capable of participation in redemption. Then He sent His Church into the world with the cross as her path, the sacraments as her nourishment, and holiness as her witness. Therefore, no Christian should imagine that pain renders him useless. Under grace, pain can become priestly and deeply fruitful for others.

The Lord says through St. Paul, "My grace is sufficient for you, for my power is made perfect in weakness" (2 Cor 12:9, RSVCE). That sentence reveals what divine grace can do through surrendered weakness. Therefore, take your suffering to the altar. Take it to confession. Take it to the Rosary. Take it into Scripture. Take it into Eucharistic adoration. Take it into the wounds of Christ. Let it become school, offering, purification, and mission. For when suffering is joined to Jesus, holiness is formed in the soul, and from that holy soul mission flows with a depth that this world can neither invent nor destroy.

Meditation Questions

1. What suffering in my life right now have I still not consciously united to the Passion of Christ?
2. When pain enters my life, do I instinctively move toward Christ, or do I first move toward distraction, resentment, self-protection, or discouragement?
3. Do I truly believe that Christ has given suffering a new meaning, and that it can become a place of communion, purification, and mission?
4. In what ways has suffering already exposed areas of pride, fear, impatience, vanity, or self-reliance in me?
5. Have I allowed hardship to make me harder, or has it begun to make me holier and more surrendered?
6. What trial in my life may actually be God's school of patience, fortitude, humility, or deeper love?
7. How has my suffering shaped the way I understand other people's wounds, burdens, and hidden battles?
8. Have I seen any way in which God has used my afflictions to make me more capable of consoling, strengthening, or serving others?

9. Do I live as though mission only happens through visible success, or do I believe that hidden sacrifice offered in union with Christ can bear real fruit for souls?
10. In my state of life, what would it look like to carry suffering with greater faith, greater peace, and greater intentional offering?
11. Have I brought my suffering fully into the sacramental life of the Church through confession, the Eucharist, prayer, and if needed the Anointing of the Sick?
12. What would change in me if I sincerely prayed each day, Lord Jesus, use this suffering for my holiness and for the salvation of souls?

Spiritual Call to Action

This chapter should move our souls from enduring suffering passively to offering suffering consciously.

Therefore, for the next seven days, begin each morning with this prayer:

Lord Jesus Christ,
I unite every suffering of this day to Your holy Passion.
Purify me through it, sanctify me through it,
and use it for the salvation of souls.

Then choose one particular suffering in your life right now and name it clearly before God. Do not leave it vague. It may be physical pain, grief, humiliation, anxiety, loneliness, financial strain, family difficulty, spiritual dryness, exhaustion, temptation, or hidden disappointment. Write it down. Then each day this week, deliberately offer that one trial to Christ.

Also, read one passage each day that teaches you how to suffer with God and in God. Spend time prayerfully with Isaiah 53, Psalm 34, Romans 8:18–39, 2 Corinthians 4:7–18, Colossians 1:24, Hebrews 12:1–13, and John 12:24–26. Read slowly. Stay with the words. Ask the Lord to show you how suffering, holiness, and mission meet in your life.

Next, make one concrete act each day that turns suffering outward in love. Pray for another suffering person. Write a message of encouragement. Visit someone lonely. Offer a hidden sacrifice for your family, your parish, a priest, a child, a marriage, or the conversion of a loved one. Let your pain become intercession.

Then bring your suffering into the sacramental life of the Church. Attend Mass this week with a deliberate offering of your trials during the Offertory. If serious sin has mixed itself into your response to suffering, go to confession. If sickness is grave or prolonged, consider asking for the Anointing of the Sick. Do not carry suffering apart from the Church's graces.

Finally, each evening ask yourself these two questions:

How did I carry suffering today?
Did I waste it, or did I offer it?
You may close each day with this prayer:
Lord Jesus Christ,
man of sorrows and risen Lord,
You know affliction from within.

Teach me to suffer with You and in You.
Save me from bitterness, self-pity, and useless resistance.
Give me patience in trial,
fortitude in weakness,
hope in darkness,
and love that becomes fruitful through sacrifice.
Let every cross in my life become a place of holiness
and a hidden offering for Your Church and for souls.
Amen.

Chapter 7

The Church in an Urgent Age

We live in an age of acceleration, fracture, temptation, noise, spiritual fatigue, and deep human hunger, and, therefore, the Church must remember again who she is, whose she is, why she exists, what she has received, and what she is sent to do, because when an age becomes disordered and restless and morally unstable, the answer is never for the Church to become thinner or softer or more hesitant in her own identity; Christ founded a people, sanctified a Bride, commissioned apostles, gave sacraments, entrusted doctrines, and sent the Holy Spirit so that the nations might be gathered into covenant communion with the living God through Jesus Christ.

Therefore, the Church in an urgent age must first recover a vivid consciousness of her origin. She was born from the pierced side of Christ. St. John records that when the soldier pierced Our Lord's side, "at once there came out blood and water" (Jn 19:34, RSVCE), and the Fathers saw in that flowing mystery the sacramental birth of the Church. The Catechism teaches, "The Church was born primarily of Christ's total self-giving for our salvation, anticipated in the institution of the Eucharist and fulfilled on the cross" (CCC 766). This means that the Church comes forth from sacrifice. She comes forth from covenant Blood. She comes forth from the divine love of the Son who gave Himself up for her. Consequently, when the world becomes unstable, the Church must return inwardly and liturgically and doctrinally to the Cross from which she came.

This also means that the Church can never understand herself merely sociologically. She is visible and historical and embodied and institutional, and yet she is far more than an organization struggling to maintain relevance within late modern conditions. St. Paul says that the Church is "the body of Christ" and "members of it" (1 Cor 12:27, RSVCE). He also says that Christ is "the head of the body, the church" (Col 1:18, RSVCE). The Catechism, likewise, teaches, "The Church is communion with Jesus" (CCC 787). Therefore, the Church in an urgent age must resist every temptation to define herself chiefly through managerial categories, political categories, therapeutic categories, or public relations categories. Her first truth is Christological. She belongs to Christ. She lives from Christ. She teaches Christ. She worships through Christ. She suffers with Christ. She extends the life of Christ sacramentally through history.

Preach the Full Gospel

In such an age as ours, this matters immensely because urgency tends to produce panic, and panic easily leads to distortion. Some react to cultural hostility by softening the Gospel. Others react by weaponizing the Gospel. Some want a Church that comforts without conversion. Others want a Church that fights without mercy. Yet the Church is called to neither sentimental dilution nor loveless severity. She is called to fidelity. She is called to truth spoken in charity. She is called to mercy rooted in repentance. She is called to moral seriousness grounded in divine love. St. Paul exhorts believers to be "speaking the truth in love" so that the Body may grow up into Christ (Eph 4:15, RSVCE). That phrase is luminous for every person of age. Truth without love wounds. Love without truth deceives. The Church must give both because Christ gives both.

Moreover, the Church must remember that she exists for salvation. This is obvious and yet often forgotten beneath secondary conversations. Jesus says, "Go therefore and make disciples of all nations" (Mt 28:19, RSVCE). St. Paul says that God "desires all men to be saved and to come to the knowledge of the truth" (1 Tim 2:4, RSVCE). Vatican II teaches that the Church is "in Christ like a sacrament or as a sign and instrument both of a very closely knit union with God and of the unity of the whole human race" (*Lumen Gentium* 1). Therefore, the Church in an urgent age must keep first things first. Her primary mission is not reputation management. It is not institutional survival detached from holiness. It is not political maneuvering as an end in itself. It is not endless inward maintenance. It is the glory of God and the salvation of souls through the proclamation of the Gospel, the administration of the sacraments, the formation of saints, and the gathering of humanity into Christ.

The Condition of Humanity Today

This becomes even more urgent when one considers the actual condition of the age. Human beings today are flooded with information and starved for wisdom. They are connected through devices and inwardly isolated. They are saturated with stimulation and deprived of peace. They speak constantly of identity while often lacking any stable account of human nature. They praise autonomy while living under addictions to approval, entertainment, lust, and impulse. They seek transcendence through substitutes while dismissing the God for whom they were made. St. Augustine's diagnosis is piercing: "You have made us for yourself, and our heart is restless until it rests in you" (*Confessions*, I.1.1). Restlessness has become a cultural atmosphere. Therefore, the Church must address this age not with vague uplift and not with timid ambiguity, rather with the living God, the incarnate Word, the holy sacraments, the moral law, the beauty of sanctity, and the joy of covenant communion.

Furthermore, this urgent age is marked by confusion about truth itself. Many treat truth as preference, narrative, social construction, institutional power, or emotional self-description. Yet Christianity begins with a different claim. Jesus says, "I am the way, and the truth, and the life" (Jn 14:6, RSVCE). The Church receives truth as a gift and revelation before she offers it as doctrine. The Catechism teaches that man is made for truth and "is obliged to honor and bear witness to it" (CCC 2467). Therefore, the Church in an urgent age must be unafraid of dogma. Dogma is not a burden upon freedom. It is light for the intellect and medicine for the soul. A people starved of truth will be devoured by counterfeit certainties. Thus, the Church must teach with courage, precision, and tenderness, because love for souls requires doctrinal fidelity.

At the same time, the Church must remain deeply human in her approach. Christ came for sinners, sufferers, widows, children, doubters, the sick, the ashamed, the proud, the poor, the rich, the burdened, the demonized, the broken, and the spiritually hungry. He wept at Lazarus's tomb (Jn 11:35, RSVCE). He had compassion on the crowds because they were like sheep without a shepherd (Mk 6:34, RSVCE). He welcomed the sinful woman who wept at His feet and told her, "Your faith has saved you; go in peace" (Lk 7:50, RSVCE). Therefore, the Church in an urgent age must resist becoming merely polemical, merely institutional, or merely performative. She must speak to actual persons. She must listen enough to diagnose truthfully. She must minister with patience. She must preach repentance with tears and with conviction. She must embody the tenderness of Christ without surrendering one inch of divine truth.

The Wounds of Today

This is especially important because urgent ages tend to produce wounded families, disordered loves, and fragile persons. Marriage weakens. Fatherhood thins. Motherhood is burdened or devalued. Children are catechized by screens. Men are tempted toward passivity or vice. Women are exhausted or ideologically manipulated. Sexuality becomes fragmented from covenant and fertility and permanence. In such a setting the Church must recover the household as a place of discipleship. The Second Vatican Council calls the family the "domestic church" (*Lumen Gentium* 11). The Catechism teaches that the Christian home is "the first school of Christian life" (CCC 1657). Therefore, the Church in an urgent age must strengthen marriages, support parents, form fathers and mothers, catechize children seriously, and call households back to prayer, Scripture, reverence, chastity, forgiveness, and sacramental fidelity.

Likewise, the Church must recover the sacred seriousness of worship. Urgent ages make people frantic, scattered, shallow, and noisy. The liturgy must, therefore, become ever more obviously what it truly is, namely participation in the worship of the living God through Christ the High Priest. The Catechism teaches, "In the earthly liturgy we take part in a foretaste of that heavenly liturgy" (CCC 1090). Vatican II says the liturgy is "the summit toward which the activity of the Church is directed" and "the font from which all her power flows" (*Sacrosanctum Concilium* 10). Therefore, the Church cannot treat worship casually when the age itself is spiritually disintegrating. People need reverence. They need silence. They need adoration. They need the word of God proclaimed with gravity. They need the Eucharist received with faith. They need the sacred to be unmistakably sacred. A frantic age requires liturgical depth.

The Sacrament of Penance

Moreover, the sacrament of Penance becomes especially urgent in such a time. Human beings today are full of guilt and yet often starved of repentance. They know something is wrong and yet frequently lack the categories to name sin, receive forgiveness, and begin again. They are told to self-manage, self-affirm, self-justify, self-medicate, self-express, and self-invent. Very few tell them to kneel, confess, repent, receive absolution, and walk in grace. Yet Christ says to the apostles, "If you forgive the sins of any, they are forgiven" (Jn 20:23, RSVCE). The Catechism teaches that those who approach the sacrament of Penance receive pardon from God's mercy and are reconciled with the Church (CCC 1422). Consequently, the Church in an urgent age must preach sin again, and preach mercy again, and open the confessional again with pastoral seriousness and evangelical hope.

Still more, the Church must recover the urgency of evangelization. The Gospel cannot simply be the private treasure of the already convinced. St. Paul cries, "Woe to me if I do not preach the gospel!" (1 Cor 9:16, RSVCE). St. Peter urges believers to "always be prepared to make a defense to any one who calls you to account for the hope that is in you" (1 Pet 3:15, RSVCE). St. John Paul II taught that the whole Church is permanently in a state of mission and called for a renewed proclamation in lands long marked by Christianity (*Redemptoris Missio* 3; *Novo Millennio Ineunte* 40). Therefore, the Church in an urgent age must reject spiritual introversion. She must preach in pulpits, teach in classrooms, witness in homes, speak in public square, create beautiful culture, engage law and philosophy and science and economics and art, and invite souls to conversion. Therefore, evangelization must be intentional.

Aristotle taught that every community aims at some good (*Politics*, I.1, 1252a1–7). Augustine later showed that earthly societies are finally defined by their loves (*City of God*, XIV.28). If that is so, then a civilization that ceases to love what is true and holy and beautiful will inevitably decay inwardly even if its technologies advance. The Church, therefore, serves the common good precisely by calling persons and societies back toward ordered love. She is not a decorative chaplain to civil life. She is a witness to the true order of reality. She proclaims that man is made in the image of God, that truth is knowable, that moral law is real, that sin destroys, that grace heals, that love requires sacrifice, that freedom requires virtue, and that Christ is Lord. In an urgent age, such a witness is not peripheral. It is civilizationally vital.

Christ Crucified

Nevertheless, the Church must never forget that her power is cruciform. She follows a crucified Lord. St. Paul says, "We preach Christ crucified" (1 Cor 1:23, RSVCE), and again, "I decided to know nothing among you except Jesus Christ and him crucified" (1 Cor 2:2, RSVCE). The Church conquers through witness, martyrdom, sanctity, patience, sacrament, truth, and charity. She certainly must defend the vulnerable and speak courageously in public affairs. Yet her deepest power is spiritual because her Lord reigns from a throne reached through Calvary. Therefore, the Church in an urgent age must resist the temptation to place final trust in strategy, influence, money, platforms, or political access. These may serve prudentially. They cannot save. Christ saves. Grace saves. The Gospel saves.

This also means that the Church herself must undergo purification continually. Urgent ages expose corruption, cowardice, vanity, worldliness, clerical pride, doctrinal confusion, moral collapse, and pastoral negligence. When these appear, the answer is never denial and never despair. The answer is repentance. St. Peter says, "It is time for judgment to begin with the household of God" (1 Pet 4:17, RSVCE). The Catechism teaches that the Church "clasping sinners to her bosom, at once holy and always in need of purification, follows constantly the path of penance and renewal" (CCC 827). Therefore, the Church in an urgent age must repent where she has failed, purify her witness, strengthen discipline, deepen priestly holiness, form leaders seriously, and recover the beauty of truth lived coherently. Reform without repentance becomes branding. Repentance restores credibility because it restores integrity before God.

Furthermore, the saints become especially important in such ages. They prove that holiness is possible under pressure. They reveal that fidelity can survive corruption and confusion. They show that truth can still burn in dark generations. St. Athanasius endured imperial and ecclesial turbulence. St. Catherine of Siena spoke with courage to a wounded Church. St. Charles Borromeo reformed pastoral life with zeal. St. Teresa of Calcutta entered urban misery with Eucharistic love. Their circumstances differed greatly. Their principle was one. Christ is enough, and grace is enough, and holiness is possible now. The Church in an urgent age must, therefore, hold up the saints as models of lived doctrine, embodied hope, and concrete charity. People need more than slogans. They need witnesses.

Time and Eternity

Then there is the question of time. Urgent ages create the illusion that every issue must be addressed immediately, and every crisis must receive constant attention and every believer must live in permanent reaction. Yet the Church lives by a deeper clock. She lives from liturgical time, sacramental time, biblical time, covenant time, and eschatological time. The Catechism teaches that since the Ascension "we are already at 'the last hour'" (CCC 670). This means the Church does live urgently. Yet her urgency is not frantic. It is ordered. It is watchful. It is patient and active and prayerful and mission-driven. She knows that Christ has already won and that history moves toward consummation under His reign. Therefore, she can labor intensely without surrendering to panic. She can respond quickly without becoming shallow. She can suffer deeply without losing hope.

This gives rise to a profoundly pastoral insight. Many ordinary believers in an urgent age are tired. They are battered by headlines, scandals, temptations, financial pressures, family burdens, ideological conflict, and personal wounds. Therefore, the Church must become again what she always is in Christ, namely mother, teacher, ark, household, field hospital in the deepest supernatural sense, school of sanctity, and home for repentant sinners. She must say to the exhausted soul, come home. She must say to the ashamed soul, confess and begin again. She must say to the confused soul, here is the truth. She must say to the proud soul, kneel. She must say to the grieving soul, Christ is risen. She must say to the distracted soul, adore. She must say to the complacent soul, awaken. She must say to the dying soul, hope in the mercy of God.

The Youth Must Rise Up

The Church also must recover bold confidence in the young. Urgent ages often form youth poorly and then speak of them despairingly. Yet Christ still calls the young, still gives vocations, still kindles heroic love, still raises saints from generations the world has already written off. St. Paul says to Timothy, "Let no one despise your youth" (1 Tim 4:12, RSVCE). Therefore, the Church in an urgent age must give young people doctrine, discipline, mission, beauty, reverence, demanding holiness, fatherhood, motherhood, clear moral teaching, and a reason to give away their lives for something eternal. The young do not need a weakened Gospel marketed cleverly. They need the living Christ and the full splendor of Catholic truth.

At the center of all this lies the Eucharistic Lord. The Church can endure urgent ages because Christ is with her. "Lo, I am with you always, to the close of the age" (Mt 28:20, RSVCE). The Catechism says that in the Most Blessed Sacrament "the body and blood, together with the soul and divinity, of our Lord Jesus Christ" are truly contained (CCC 1374). Therefore, the Church's answer to urgent history is not mere analysis. It is adoration. It is a sacrifice. It is sacramental communion. It is kneeling before the One who has already conquered sin and death. Every reform worthy of the name must return there. Every mission worthy of the Gospel must proceed from there. Every urgent age must be interpreted under the light that shines from the altar.

And so the Church in an urgent age must be more fully herself. More prayerful. More sacramental. More doctrinally faithful. More pastorally tender. More morally serious. More evangelically bold. More contemplative. More missionary. More rooted in Scripture. More alive in the liturgy. More honest in repentance. More radiant in holiness. She must not shrink. She must not drift. She must not forget her origin in the side of Christ, her nourishment in the Eucharist, her authority in divine revelation, her strength in the Holy Spirit, and her destiny in the heavenly Jerusalem. For the age is urgent indeed, and precisely for that reason the Church must again become unmistakably the Church of Jesus Christ.

Meditation Questions

1. Do I truly see the Church as born from the pierced side of Christ and living from His sacrifice, or have I allowed myself to think of her chiefly in human, political, cultural, or institutional terms?
2. In this urgent age, where have I been tempted toward fear, cynicism, bitterness, or discouragement about the Church?
3. Do I love the Church as the Body of Christ and the Bride of Christ, even while recognizing her wounds, weaknesses, and need for purification?
4. Have I expected the Church to conform herself to the age rather than call the age to conversion?
5. In what ways have I contributed to the strengthening of the Church in my own home, parish, friendships, and public witness, and in what ways have I remained passive?
6. Do I approach the liturgy and the sacraments as the living heart of the Church's response to a fractured age, or have I treated them too casually?
7. Have I allowed the confusion of the age to weaken my confidence in truth, or have I remained rooted in Christ who says, "I am the way, and the truth, and the life" (John 14:6)?
8. How seriously do I take the Church's mission to save souls, proclaim the Gospel, and form saints?
9. Am I praying for priests, bishops, families, young people, and the renewal of the Church with real perseverance?
10. In what ways has the age formed me more deeply than the Church has formed me?

11. Have I become more reactive than prayerful, more agitated than faithful, more opinionated than holy?
12. What would it mean for me personally to help the Church become more visibly prayerful, reverent, truthful, charitable, and missionary in this urgent age?

Spiritual Call to Action

Knowing these truths should lead us to a renewed fidelity to the Church in a time of confusion, fatigue, and spiritual hunger. Therefore, the call to action here is simple and concrete: strengthen the Church first in yourself, then in your home, then in the place where God has planted you.

For the next seven days, begin each day with this prayer: Lord Jesus Christ, make me a faithful son within Your Church in this urgent age. Purify my heart, strengthen my hope, and make me useful for the renewal of Your people.

Then choose one act each day that deepens your communion with the Church. Attend Mass if possible. Pray for your parish priest by name. Read one passage from the Gospels and one paragraph from the Catechism. Pray a decade of the Rosary for bishops and priests. Make a visit to the Blessed Sacrament. Offer a sacrifice for the conversion of souls. Let each day include one deliberate act of ecclesial fidelity.

Also, examine how the spirit of the age has shaped you. Look honestly at your use of media, your speech about the Church, your reverence at Mass, your seriousness about confession, your love for truth, and your willingness to evangelize. Write down three areas where the culture has influenced you more than Christ has, and next to each one write one concrete step of correction.

Then make one act this week that strengthens the Church in your actual surroundings. Encourage a fallen-away Catholic to return to Mass. Invite someone to confession or Eucharistic adoration. Begin family prayer in your home. Offer practical support to your parish. Share a faithful Catholic book, talk, or Scripture passage with someone who needs it. The Church is strengthened through real acts of fidelity.

If you have been spiritually discouraged by scandal, confusion, or weakness within the Church, bring that discouragement directly before Christ in prayer and say aloud: Jesus, Your Church is Yours before she is mine. Keep me faithful, hopeful, reverent, and steadfast within her.

Finally, spend time this week before the Eucharist, whether at Mass or in adoration, and consciously place the whole Church before the Lord: her holiness, her wounds, her shepherds, her families, her young people, her sinners, her saints, and her mission in the world.

You may close each day with this prayer:

Lord Jesus Christ,
You founded Your Church through Your saving sacrifice
and You remain with her to the close of the age.
Keep me from fear, bitterness, cynicism, and passivity.
Root me more deeply in Your truth,
Your sacraments,
Your mission,

and Your holy presence.
Purify Your Church, strengthen Your priests,
sanctify Your people,
and make me faithful in this urgent age.
May my life help reveal the beauty of Your Bride
to a weary and wounded world.
Amen.

Chapter 8

This Is the Hour

This is the hour because Christ has already entered His hour, and once He has entered it through crucifixion, Resurrection, and Ascension, every other hour in human history receives its truest meaning from Him, so that time itself is no longer morally neutral or spiritually undefined or safely open to indefinite delay; the Son of God has acted decisively within history and has drawn the human race into the crisis and mercy of covenant fulfillment. Hence, this is the hour for repentance. This is the hour for faith. This is the hour for surrender. This is the hour for holiness. This is the hour for courage. This is the hour to belong wholly to Jesus Christ.

At the beginning of this book, we considered the language of the hour in the Gospel of John. Jesus says at Cana, "My hour has not yet come" (Jn 2:4, RSVCE). Later St. John says that hostile men could not seize Him "because his hour had not yet come" (Jn 7:30, RSVCE). Then, as the shadow of the Cross lengthens, Jesus declares, "The hour has come for the Son of man to be glorified" (Jn 12:23, RSVCE). That is where everything changed forever. The hour of Christ was the hour of covenant sacrifice, the hour of divine love poured out unto death, the hour of judgment upon sin, the hour of victory over the ruler of this world, the hour of Resurrection, the hour of heavenly enthronement. Thus, the hour of Jesus was never merely His private destiny. It was the decisive turning of the ages. It was the dawn of the world renewed in Him.

Consequently, the human soul now lives in a new condition before God. The Christ who was crucified is risen. The Christ who was risen is ascended. The Christ who ascended now reigns and intercedes. The Catechism teaches, "Since the Ascension God's plan has entered into its fulfillment. We are already at 'the last hour'" (CCC 670). That sentence should pierce through every layer of spiritual delay and religious drift. We are already at the last hour. History is already charged with eschatological seriousness. The King has taken His throne. The Spirit has been poured out. The Gospel has gone into the nations. The Church has been born from the side of Christ. Therefore, Christian life belongs to the decisive age of salvation.

The Final Temptation

This means that the final temptation of many believers is to admire the Gospel without actually yielding to it in full. One can admire Calvary and still withhold repentance. One can affirm the Resurrection and still live timidly. One can profess the Ascension and still stay spiritually earthbound. One can even love the Church and still drift into passivity. Yet the hour of Christ destroys every safe distance. It lays claim upon the whole person. St. Paul writes, "Behold, now is the acceptable time; behold, now is the day of salvation" (2 Cor 6:2, RSVCE). He does not say that now is the day for mild religious interest. He does not say that now is the day for gradual indefinite openness. He says now is the day of salvation. Therefore, this is the hour because grace has already made its claim.

Moreover, this hour is personal. Christ did not die for a faceless humanity in the abstract. St. Paul says, "The Son of God… loved me and gave himself for me" (Gal 2:20, RSVCE). Those words should stop us in our tracks. He loved me. He gave Himself for me. The Cross is, therefore, no distant spectacle. The empty tomb is no merely communal symbol. The Ascension is no remote theological category. All of it presses toward personal communion. Jesus calls souls by name just as He called Mary Magdalene by name near the garden tomb, "Mary" (Jn 20:16, RSVCE). Therefore, the question at this point is not simply whether the Gospel is true in a general way. The question is whether you will answer the One who has loved you unto the end.

This is also the hour because the heart is always being formed. No soul stays fixed in spiritual neutrality. Aristotle saw that we become what we repeatedly do, and that virtue arises through habituation (Nicomachean Ethics, II.1, 1103a14–26). St. Thomas Aquinas, receiving and elevating this insight within Christian theology, teaches that habits shape the powers of the soul toward certain acts (Summa Theologiae, I-II, q. 49, a. 3; q. 51, a. 2). Therefore, every day is formative. Every indulgence forms. Every act of prayer forms. Every delay forms. Every surrender forms. Every confession forms. Every compromise forms. The soul is always becoming someone. Consequently, this is the hour because your life is already moving toward holiness or away from it through countless real choices.

Our Life is Limited

At the same time, Scripture gives repeated warnings against imagining that time is endlessly available. "Today, when you hear his voice, do not harden your hearts" (Heb 3:7–8, RSVCE). "Seek the

Lord while he may be found, call upon him while he is near" (Is 55:6, RSVCE). "Watch therefore, for you know neither the day nor the hour" (Mt 25:13, RSVCE). "You are a mist that appears for a little time and then vanishes" (Jas 4:14, RSVCE). These texts do not speak in order to create panic. They speak in order to create sobriety. They call the soul out of illusion and into truth. Time is a gift. It is not possession. Breath is given. It is not guaranteed. Therefore, this is the hour because tomorrow has never been ours to command.

Yet my point here is not merely about danger. It is even more about possibility through grace. Christ summons us because He desires our life. "I came that they may have life, and have it abundantly" (Jn 10:10, RSVCE). The Father commands repentance because He delights in sons returning home. The prodigal's father runs toward his son, embraces him, clothes him, restores him, and rejoices over him (Lk 15:20–24, RSVCE). Therefore, this is the hour because mercy is open now. The Blood of the Covenant still speaks. The confessional is still open. The altar is still set. The Spirit still convicts. The Church still teaches. Christ still calls.

Accordingly, this hour must be understood covenantally. In Scripture covenant is never mere sentiment. It is sacred belonging. It is oath-bound fidelity. It is a relational bond established by divine initiative and sealed in sacrifice. At Sinai Moses said, "Behold the blood of the covenant" (Ex 24:8, RSVCE). In the upper room Jesus says, "This is my blood of the covenant, which is poured out for many" (Mk 14:24, RSVCE). Therefore, the Christian lives under covenant Blood. He belongs to a people gathered by sacrifice and fed by sacrifice. He is baptized into Christ's death and Resurrection. The Catechism teaches that Baptism makes us members of Christ and partakers of the divine nature (CCC 1265–1267). Hence this is the hour because covenant life demands covenant fidelity.

Holiness Isn't Optional

This also means that holiness can never be an optional enhancement to ordinary Christianity. Vatican II says, "All the faithful of Christ of whatever rank or status are called to the fullness of the Christian life and to the perfection of charity" (Lumen Gentium 40). The universal call to holiness is not a devotional slogan. It is the ordinary meaning of baptismal life. Therefore, this is the hour to reject mediocrity. It is the hour to reject lukewarmness. It is the hour to reject the thought that sanctity belongs to other souls in other centuries under easier conditions. The risen Christ still sanctifies His people now. He still calls men and women, married and single, priest and layman, young and old, exhausted and eager, wounded and strong, into the fullness of charity.

Furthermore, this is the hour because the world itself is aching for a witness that is unmistakably Christian. Our age is full of noise and inward emptiness. It is full of stimulation and spiritual malnourishment. It is full of language about identity and severe confusion about what man is. It is full of longing for love and great fear of covenant. It is full of therapeutic speech and little repentance. It is full of self-expression and little self-gift. Therefore, the hour is urgent because the age is urgent. The Church must shine with greater holiness, stronger doctrine, deeper reverence, clearer moral witness, truer mercy, and more joyful confidence. Yet the Church shines only through actual Christians. She shines through fathers who pray and lead and repent. She shines through mothers who nurture and teach and persevere. She shines through priests who preach, sacrifice, absolve, and shepherd with purity. She shines through consecrated souls who reveal the beauty of total belonging. She shines through ordinary believers who live the Gospel seriously in hidden places.

This Is The Hour

In this sense, this is the hour for the home. Families cannot outsource Christian formation to institutions while domestic life is spiritually unguarded. "As for me and my house, we will serve the Lord" (Josh 24:15, RSVCE). The Christian household must again become a place of prayer, reverence, truthfulness, chastity, forgiveness, catechesis, Scripture, and sacramental preparation. The Catechism calls the family "the first school of Christian life" and "a school for human enrichment" (CCC 1657, 2207). Therefore, this is the hour for fathers to act like fathers and mothers to act like mothers and children to be formed in the fear of the Lord. The age will catechize every household somehow. The Christian household must, therefore, choose whom it will serve.

It is also the hour for worship. A distracted civilization requires reverent liturgy. A wounded people require sacred medicine. An anxious generation requires adoration. The Eucharist is "the source and summit of the Christian life" (CCC 1324). Christ is truly present, body and blood, soul and divinity, in the Most Blessed Sacrament (CCC 1374). Therefore, this is the hour to return to Sunday with seriousness, to kneel again with faith, to confess again with honesty, to receive Holy Communion with awe, to adore again in silence, and to let the liturgy shape the whole rhythm of life. The altar is not one spiritual option among many. It is where the Church lives from the sacrifice of her Lord.

Likewise, this is the hour for truth. "You will know the truth, and the truth will make you free" (Jn 8:32, RSVCE). An age that doubts truth cannot heal itself by cleverer slogans or softer dogma. It needs revelation. It needs the Word made flesh. It needs the Church to teach with courage and tenderness. The Catechism says, "Man tends by nature toward the truth" (CCC 2467). Therefore, this is the hour to study Scripture seriously, to know the faith deeply, to reject sentimental ignorance, to form conscience under divine law, to think Christianly about body and soul and marriage and suffering and salvation and judgment and heaven and hell. Charity without truth dissolves into sentiment. Truth without charity hardens into pride. The Church must offer both because Christ gives both, and every believer must receive both with humility.

Still more, this is the hour for repentance. Every chapter of this book has been moving toward that inner word. Repentance is not humiliation for its own sake. It is the doorway into freedom. It is truth-telling before mercy. It is the prodigal rising. It is Peter weeping and returning. It is David crying, "Create in me a clean heart, O God" (Ps 51:10, RSVCE). It is the tax collector beating his breast and saying, "God, be merciful to me a sinner!" (Lk 18:13, RSVCE). The Catechism teaches that interior repentance is a radical reorientation of the whole life, a return to God with all the heart (CCC 1431). Therefore, this is the hour to name the sin, abandon the excuse, go to confession, repair the harm, cut off the near occasion, and begin again in grace.

And this is the hour for courage. The apostles after Pentecost became bold witnesses. "We cannot but speak of what we have seen and heard" (Acts 4:20, RSVCE). Courage is needed now in families, schools, parishes, media, law, business, and public life. Courage is needed to speak the truth about marriage, sexuality, dignity, justice, worship, sin, mercy, and salvation. Courage is needed to be faithful when misunderstood. Courage is needed to endure mockery without softening divine truth. Yet Christian courage is never bluster. It grows from union with Christ. It is born from prayer, sacrifice, truth, and hope. Thus, this is the hour for witness, and witness begins by belonging wholly to the Lord.

What Are Our Loves?

Augustine teaches that two loves have built two cities, the earthly city through love of self unto contempt of God, and the heavenly city through love of God unto self-forgetfulness (City of God, XIV.28). Every hour of life contributes to one city or the other. Every use of time, every shaping of desire, every ordering of home, every moral choice, every political act, every word spoken, every habit embraced, every prayer prayed is a kind of citizenship. Therefore, this is the hour because your life is building toward one city or the other already. The Christian must choose the City of God with deliberate and renewed fidelity.

Yet beneath all this seriousness there is still a profound sweetness. Christ summons us into urgency because joy is found on the far side of surrender. "These things I have spoken to you, that my joy may be in you, and that your joy may be full" (Jn 15:11, RSVCE).

The saints are not grim monuments of religious effort. They are men and women in whom love has become integrated, purified, and luminous. Therefore, this is the hour to stop bargaining with half-measures. It is the hour to discover the joy of full belonging. It is the hour to discover that holiness is severe only toward what destroys us and tender toward what heals us. It is the hour to discover that the commandments protect freedom and that grace empowers what nature alone cannot sustain.

Dear friend, if this book has done anything worthwhile, it has brought you again to the person of Jesus Christ. He is the one who entered the hour. He is the one who loved you on the Cross. He is the one who conquered death. He is the one who ascended in glory. He is the one who founded the Church. He is the one who calls you now. Therefore, I end with a summons. Christ is asking for your whole life. He is asking for your heart, your habits, your speech, your imagination, your work, your family, your body, your prayer, your grief, your wounds, your future, your hidden loyalties, your unspoken fears, your plans, your money, your friendships, your vocation, your time. He is asking for all of it because He has redeemed all of it.

So then, this is the hour:

This is the hour to kneel.
This is the hour to confess.
This is the hour to believe.
This is the hour to forgive.
This is the hour to reorder the home.
This is the hour to sanctify Sunday.

This is the hour to return to Scripture.
This is the hour to deepen prayer.
This is the hour to leave grave sin.
This is the hour to break lukewarmness.
This is the hour to speak the Gospel.
This is the hour to repair what has been neglected.
This is the hour to become serious about heaven.
This is the hour to live and die as one who belongs to Jesus Christ.

The Church teaches that death ends the time open to accepting or rejecting the grace manifested in Christ (CCC 1021). That sober truth is not given to terrify the faithful into paralysis. It is given to awaken them into love. Since time is finite and grace is present and Christ is reigning, the only fitting answer is prompt fidelity. "Today, when you hear his voice, do not harden your hearts" (Heb 3:15, RSVCE). Therefore, answer Him today. Love Him today. Return today. Begin today. The hour of His saving work has already come. Your hour to answer Him is now.

Meditation Questions

1. When I hear the words "This is the hour," do I receive them as a living summons from Christ, or merely as a stirring idea?
2. What specific part of my life is Christ asking me to surrender fully right now?
3. Have I truly allowed the Cross, the Resurrection, and the Ascension to shape the way I use my time, order my priorities, and judge what matters most?

4. Where am I still living as though tomorrow is guaranteed and today's obedience can wait?
5. In what ways have I admired the Gospel while resisting its full claim upon my heart?
6. What habits in me are building the City of God, and what habits are quietly building the earthly city?
7. Is my home becoming more visibly Christian in prayer, reverence, truth, and sacramental life, or has the spirit of the age shaped it more deeply than Christ has?
8. Do I truly believe that holiness is meant for me now, in my present state of life, in my present responsibilities, in my present weaknesses?
9. What sin, compromise, distraction, fear, resentment, or attachment must I leave behind if I am to answer Christ seriously in this hour?
10. How has Christ been calling me personally through this book, and what have I sensed most strongly in prayer or conscience?
11. If this really is the decisive hour of grace in my life, what would wholehearted fidelity look like in the next week?
12. When I stand before Christ, what response do I want to have given to His love in this present hour?

Spiritual Call to Action

This final chapter should end with us offering a decisive response. The whole book has been moving toward this: answer Christ now.

Therefore, within the next twenty-four hours, make one concrete act of total seriousness before God. Kneel before a crucifix or before the Blessed Sacrament and speak to Jesus plainly. Tell Him what in your life must change. Name what you are surrendering. Name what you are leaving behind. Name what you are asking for. Do not speak vaguely. Speak personally.

Then, make a written response to the Lord under this title: **This Is the Hour**. Write one page only. Include three things:

- First, what Christ has shown you through this book.
- Second, what you must repent of.
- Third, what you will now do in response. Keep it simple, direct, and honest.

Also, within the next seven days, do these four things:

1) Go to confession, attend Mass with serious preparation, set one fixed daily time for prayer, and remove one recurring source of spiritual compromise from your life. Let these four actions become your first concrete answer to grace.
2) Next, choose one area from each of these categories and act on it this week: prayer, family, morality, and mission.

   For prayer, deepen one's practice.

   For family, strengthen one act of leadership, forgiveness, or spiritual fidelity.

   For morality, cut off one sinful pattern or near occasion of sin.

   For mission, speak one word for Christ to another person.

3) Then, reclaim Sunday deliberately. Prepare for it the day before. Protect it from unnecessary distraction. Enter Mass reverently. Give time to rest, prayer, Scripture, and spiritual recollection. Let the Lord's Day become the weekly anchor of your answer to Christ.
4) Finally, pray this each day for the next week:

Lord Jesus Christ,
You entered Your hour for my salvation.
You were crucified for me,
You rose in glory,
and You ascended to the Father's right hand.
This is the hour for my response.
Take my heart, my habits, my thoughts, my home, my desires, my fears, and my future.
Save me from delay, compromise, and half-heartedness.
Teach me to live wholly for You,
faithfully in Your Church,
firmly in Your truth,
and joyfully in Your grace.
Let my life become a sincere answer
to Your covenant love.
Amen.

Spiritual Checklist

This is a spiritual checklist that may be used as an examination of conscience to compel us to a more committed decision of living "the Hour."

1. Have I truly received that Christ's Cross was for me personally, and that His Blood was poured out for my salvation?
2. Do I live each day with conscious gratitude for the Resurrection of Jesus Christ?
3. Have I allowed the Ascension of Christ to shape my understanding of heaven, mission, and hope?
4. Do I still treat time as though I have endless chances to repent later?
5. Is there any grave sin, habitual compromise, or hidden indulgence I have continued to protect?
6. Am I lukewarm in prayer, worship, or moral effort?
7. Do I approach Sunday Mass as the center of my week and the center of my identity?
8. Have I delayed confession through pride, shame, laziness, or spiritual dullness?
9. Do I pray every day with real intentionality, or only when I feel pressure or need?
10. Is Sacred Scripture truly shaping my mind, or am I more deeply formed by media, noise, and the spirit of the age?
11. Have I surrendered my body, speech, imagination, and desires to the lordship of Christ?

12. Do I love the Church as the Body and Bride of Christ, even amid her wounds and need for purification?
13. Am I actively helping strengthen the Church in my home, parish, friendships, and witness?
14. Do I see suffering as something to unite to Christ, or only as something to escape?
15. Have I offered my present sufferings for my holiness and for the salvation of souls?
16. Am I living my vocation with covenant seriousness, whether in marriage, priesthood, single life, consecrated life, or friendship?
17. Have I allowed my home to become spiritually passive, distracted, and under-formed?
18. Do I regularly examine my conscience with honesty before God?
19. Have I forgiven those who have wounded me, or am I still nursing bitterness?
20. Do I speak openly about Christ when appropriate, or do I hide my faith to remain comfortable?
21. Am I raising my family, if I have one, with deliberate prayer, truth, reverence, and sacramental fidelity?
22. Have I mistaken admiration of the Gospel for obedience to the Gospel?
23. Is there a concrete act of repentance, reconciliation, or surrender that I already know I need to make?
24. If Christ were to call me from this life sooner than I expect, would I be at peace with the state of my soul?

25. Can I truthfully say that Jesus Christ is the center of my life, rather than an important part of it?

Ten Concrete Steps to Live this Book

1. Establish a fixed daily prayer time

   Choose one non-negotiable time each day, even fifteen to twenty minutes, and keep it faithfully. Read Scripture, pray honestly, and place the day under Christ's lordship.

2. Return Sunday to its rightful place

   Prepare for Mass the day before. Arrive early. Recollect yourself. Receive the Eucharist reverently. Protect Sunday from needless distraction and let it become the weekly anchor of your soul.

3. Go to confession regularly

   Do not wait for spiritual collapse. Make confession a normal part of Christian vigilance. Monthly confession is a strong and practical rhythm for many souls.

4. Remove one recurring source of compromise

   Identify one concrete source of spiritual weakness, whether it is media, impurity, gossip, resentment, laziness, or distraction, and cut it off deliberately.

5. Begin a nightly examen

   Each evening ask: Where did I respond to grace today? Where did I resist it? Where do I need mercy? This builds spiritual honesty and readiness.

6. Make your suffering an offering

   When sorrow, fatigue, humiliation, illness, or frustration comes, consciously unite it to Christ's Passion and offer it for your holiness and for the salvation of souls.

7. Bring prayer into the home

   Pray aloud in your home. Read Scripture together. Bless meals with intention. Keep sacred images visible. Let your household become recognizably Christian.

8. Study the faith seriously

   Read the Gospels, the Catechism, and one solid Catholic book regularly. A serious age requires serious formation. Do not remain spiritually undereducated.

9. Make one concrete act of witness each week

   Invite someone to Mass, share a Scripture passage, encourage a fallen-away Catholic, speak truth charitably, or offer to pray with someone. Let your faith move outward.

10. Live with the urgency of today

    Each morning say: This is the hour to belong wholly to Christ. Then act accordingly. Repent quickly. Obey promptly. Forgive readily. Pray sincerely. Begin now.

My Resolution Before God

Because Jesus Christ was crucified for me,
because He rose in glory,
because He ascended and reigns,
I will no longer live casually, delay repentance,
or treat grace lightly.

I will live this hour for Christ,
in His Church,
through prayer,
the sacraments,
truth,
sacrifice,
and mission.
By His grace, I will begin now.

www.ingramcontent.com/pod-product-compliance
Lightning Source LLC
LaVergne TN
LVHW040221110826
845146LV00005B/1365